"A lovely little book that contains gems about the writing process . . . A fine addition to the pantheon of writing life guides that includes Brenda Ueland's *If You Want to Write*, Annie Dillard's *The Writing Life*, and Anne Lamott's *Bird by Bird*."

—*Library Journal* (starred review)

"Honest and conversational, Shapiro provides an introspective look into the creative process and the value of persistence, offering insight to writers at any level." —*Booklist*

"A thoughtful examination of [Shapiro's] life and the creative process that has defined it. . . . Cleareyed, honest and grounded."

—*Kirkus Reviews*

"*Still Writing* offers up a cornucopia of wisdom, insights, and practical lessons gleaned from Dani Shapiro's long experience as a celebrated writer and teacher of writing. The beneficiaries are beginning writers, veteran writers, and everyone in between." —Jennifer Egan

"Writers need hope. Writers need help. Thank you, Dani Shapiro."
—Michael Cunningham

"Dani Shapiro has written a wise, pragmatic, and soulful field guide to the writing life. *Still Writing* is filled with honest words to not only live by but write toward. Shapiro has created a well-drawn map for the lost, the weary, and the found. I loved it."

—Terry Tempest Williams

"One of those rare books that is both beautiful and useful. *Still Writing* is an exploration of the writing life, lit up by Shapiro's luminous voice." —Susan Orlean

"Dani Shapiro's novels and nonfiction are always rich in honesty and intelligence, about the psyche and lost hearts and families, about messes and shame and what calls us to transcend; and how painfully we find out who we are, and how inadequate and stunning the journey is, how it goes both so slowly and in the blink of an eye—how dark and then what (against all odds) so brilliantly lights the way."

—Anne Lamott

STILL WRITING

The Pleasures and Perils of a Creative Life

By Dani Shapiro

Grove Press
New York

Published simultaneously in Canada
Printed in the United States of America

ISBN 978-0-8021-2141-7
ISBN 978-0-8021-9343-8

Grove Press
an imprint of Grove/Atlantic, Inc.
154 West 14th Street
New York, NY 10011

Distributed by Publishers Group West

www.groveatlantic.com

14 15 16 17   10 9 8 7 6 5 4 3 2 1

In Memory of Grace Paley

"I have to get lost so I can invent some way out."

—David Salle

STILL WRITING

The Pleasures and Perils of a Creative Life

INTRODUCTION

I've heard it said that everything you need to know about life can be learned from watching baseball. I'm not what you'd call a sports fan, so I don't know if this is true, but I do believe in a similar philosophy, which is that everything you need to know about life can be learned from a genuine and ongoing attempt to write.

At least this has been the case for me.

I have been writing all my life. Growing up, I wrote in soft-covered journals, in spiral-bound notebooks, in diaries with locks and keys. I wrote love letters and lies, stories and missives. When I wasn't writing, I was reading. And when I wasn't writing or reading, I was staring out the window, lost in thought. Life was elsewhere—I was sure of it—and writing was what took me there. In my notebooks, I escaped an un-happy and lonely childhood. I tried to make sense of myself. I had no intention of becoming a writer. I didn't know that becoming a writer was possible. Still, writing was what saved me. It presented me with a window into the infinite. It allowed me to create order out of chaos.

Of course, there's a huge difference between the scribblings of a young girl in her journals—I would never get out from under my bed if anyone were ever to read them—and the sustained, grown-up work of crafting something resonant and lasting, a story that might shed light on our human condition. "The good writer," Ralph Waldo Emerson noted in his journal, "seems to be writing about himself, but has his eye always on that thread of the universe which runs through himself and all things."

Sitting down to write isn't easy. A few years ago, a local high school asked me if a student who is interested in becoming a writer might come and observe me. Observe me! I had to decline. I couldn't imagine what the poor student would think, watching me sit, then stand, sit again, decide that I needed more coffee, go downstairs and make the coffee, come back up, sit again, get up, comb my hair, sit again, stare at the screen, check e-mail, stand up, pet the dog, sit again . . .

You get the picture.

The writing life requires courage, patience, persistence, empathy, openness, and the ability to deal with rejection. It requires the willingness to be alone with oneself. To be gentle with oneself. To look at the world without blinders on. To observe and withstand what one sees. To be disciplined, and at the same time, take risks. To be willing to fail—not just once, but again and again, over the course of a lifetime. "Ever tried, ever failed," Samuel Beckett once wrote. "No matter. Try again. Fail again. Fail better." It requires what the great editor Ted Solotoroff once called *endurability*. It is this quality, most of all, that I think of when I look around a classroom at a group of aspiring writers. Some of them will be more gifted than others. Some of them will be driven, ambitious for success or fame, rather than by the determination to do their best possible work. But of the students I have taught, it is not necessarily the most gifted, or the ones most focused on imminent literary fame (I think of these as short sprinters), but the ones who endure, who are still writing, decades later.

It is my hope that—whether you're a writer or not—this book will help you to discover or rediscover the qualities necessary for a creative life. We are all unsure of ourselves. Every one of us walking the planet wonders, secretly, if we are getting it wrong. We stumble along. We love and we lose. At times, we find unexpected strength, and at other times, we succumb to our fears. We are impatient. We want to know what's around the corner, and the writing life won't offer us this. It forces us into the here and now. There is only this moment, when we put pen to page.

Had I not, as a young woman, discovered that I was a writer, had I not met some extraordinarily generous role models and teachers and mentors who helped me along the way, had I not begun to forge a path out of my own personal wilderness with words, I might not be here to tell this story. I was spinning, whirling, without any sense of who I was, or what I was made of. I was slowly, quietly killing myself. But after writing saved my life, the practice of it also became my teacher. It is impossible to spend your days writing and not begin to know your own mind.

The page is your mirror. What happens inside you is reflected back. You come face-to-face with your own resistance, lack of balance, self-loathing, and insatiable ego—and also with your singular vision, guts, and fortitude. No matter what you've achieved the day before, you begin each day at the bottom of the mountain. Isn't this true for most of us? A surgeon about to perform a difficult operation is at the bottom of the mountain. A lawyer delivering a closing argument. An actor waiting in the wings. A teacher on the first day of school. Sometimes we may think that we're in charge, or that we have things figured out. Life is usually right there, though, ready to knock us over when we get too sure of ourselves. Fortunately, if we have learned the lessons that years of practice have taught us, when this happens, we endure. We fail better. We sit up, dust ourselves off, and begin again.

"Endings are elusive, middles are nowhere to be found, but worst of all is to begin, to begin, to begin!"

—Donald Barthelme

SCARS

I grew up the only child of older parents. If I were to give you a list of all the facts of my early life that made me a writer, this one would be near the top. *Only child. Older parents.* It now almost seems like a job requirement—though back then, I wished it to be otherwise. A lonely, isolated childhood isn't a prerequisite for a writing life, of course, but it certainly helped. My parents were observant Jews. We kept a kosher home. On the Sabbath, from sundown on Friday evening until sundown on Saturday, we didn't drive, we didn't turn on lights, or the radio, or television, and I wasn't allowed to ride my bike, or play the piano, or do homework. This left me with a lot of time to do nothing. Most Saturday mornings, I walked a half-mile to synagogue with my father while my mother stayed home with a sinus headache.

Our house was silent and spotless. Dirt, smudges, noise—any kind of disarray would have been unthinkable. House-keepers were always quitting. No one could keep the house to my mother's standards. Every surface gleamed. Picture frames were dusted daily. Sheets and pillowcases were ironed three times a week. My drawers were color-coordinated: blue

Danskin tops perfectly folded next to blue Danskin bottoms. The exterminator came monthly. The toxic mold guy made biannual visits. Summers, the lawn man came every few days with his mower and hedge trimmer, clipping our suburban New Jersey acre into shape.

Control was important. It wasn't the messiness of life that we were girding ourselves against. Secrets floated through our home like dust motes in the air. Every word spoken by my parents contained within it a hidden hard kernel of what wasn't being said. Though I couldn't have expressed it, I knew with a child's instincts that life was seen by both my parents as a teeming, seething, frightful hall of mirrors. Something had made them scared. They tried to protect me from themselves, from their own histories—*das kind,* one of them would whisper harshly and they'd stop talking after I entered the room. I loved my parents, but I didn't want to be like them. I didn't want to be afraid of life. The trouble was, their way was all I knew.

And so I spent my childhood straining to hear. With no siblings to distract me, I had plenty of time, and eavesdropped and snooped in every way I could devise. I lurked outside doorways, crouched on staircase landings. I fiddled with the intercom system in our house, attempting to tune in to rooms where one or both of my parents might be. I riffled through filing cabinets when my parents were out to dinner and the babysitter was downstairs watching "The Partridge Family." I haunted my mother's closets—the cashmere sweaters in individual plastic garment bags, the shoes and purses in their original boxes. What was I hoping to find? A clue. A *reason*. We had telephones in almost every room, but the one in my mother's office had a little doohickey that you could lift up, preventing anyone from picking up another extension, and listening in. I noticed that whenever my mother was on the phone, she used it. What was she saying that I wasn't meant to hear?

I didn't know that this spying was the beginning of my literary education. That the need to know, to discover, to peel away the surface was a training ground for who and what I would grow up to become. The idea of becoming a writer was more remote to me than becoming an astronaut. I didn't know any writers. Our neighborhood wasn't an artistic hotbed. I didn't draw parallels between the books I loved, and read every night under the covers with a flashlight, and the idea that someone—a woman, say, alone in a room, wrestling with words and thoughts and ideas—could in fact spend her life writing them.

I slunk around like a detective. I learned to hide on the staircase without making a sound. I wanted to unearth the sources of my parents' pain, though it would be many years before I would begin to understand it. All I knew was this: life seemed sad. It seemed parched, fruitless, devoid of joy. By the time I was eleven or twelve, I began to escape into my room and to write. I discovered my imagination, where I was free of my father's sorrow, my mother's headaches. I was free from the sense that my parents were disappointed in each other, and from my fear that they would be disappointed in me. I was free from *das kind!*, and the Sabbath rules. I closed and locked my bedroom door—take *that,* parents!—and I made up stories. Sometimes I wrote them as letters to friends. Sometimes I pretended every word was true.

I wondered if I might be crazy.

I had no idea that I was becoming a writer.

RIDING THE WAVE

Here's a short list of what not to do when you sit down to write. Don't answer the phone. Don't look at e-mail. Don't go on the Internet for any reason, including checking the spelling of some obscure word, or for what you might think of as research but is really a fancy form of procrastination. Do you need to know, right this minute, the exact make and year of the car your character is driving? Do you need to know which exit on the interstate has a rest stop? Can it wait? It can almost always wait. On the list of other, less fancy procrastinations, when your wild surge of energy is accompanied by the urge to leap up from your desk, are: laundry, baking, marketing, filling out insurance claims, writing thank-you notes, cleaning closets, sorting files, weeding, scrubbing, polishing, arranging, removing stains, bathing the dog.

Sit down. Stay there. It's hard—I know just how hard—and I hate to tell you this, but it doesn't get easier. Ever. Get used to the discomfort. Make some kind of peace with it. Several years ago, I decided to learn how to meditate, though I thought, as many do, that I'd be bad at it: *I'm too type A. I can't sit still.* But I needed something that, when I did get up from my desk, would bring me peace and clarity. All of my writer friends have rituals: my friend Jenny runs. John cooks barbecue. Mary swims. Ann knits. These are meditative acts—ones that allow the mind to roam, and ultimately to rest. When I sit down to meditate, I feel much the same way I do when I sit down to write: resistant, fidgety, anxious, eager, cranky, despairing, hopeful, my mind jammed so full of ideas, my heart so full of feelings that it seems impossible to contain them. And yet . . . if I do just sit there without checking the clock, without answering the ringing phone, without jumping up to make a note of an all-important task, then slowly the random thoughts pinging around my mind begin to settle. If I allow myself, I begin to see more clearly what's going on. Like a snow globe, that flurry of white floats down.

During the time devoted to your writing, think of the surges of energy coursing through your body as waves. They will come, they will crash over you, and then they will go. You'll still be sitting there. Nothing terrible will have happened. Try not to run from the wave. If, at one moment, you are sitting quietly at your desk, and then—fugue state alert!—you are suddenly on your knees planting tulips, or perusing your favorite online shopping Web site, and you don't know how you got there, then the wave has won. We don't want the wave to win. We want to recognize it, accept its power, and even learn to ride it. We want to learn to withstand those wild surges, because everything we need to know, everything valuable, is contained within them.

INNER CENSOR

Sometimes, when I'm teaching, I'll start to talk to my students about the nasty little two-timing frenemy of everyone who struggles to put words down on the page—and, without even realizing I'm doing it, I'll start gesturing to my left shoulder. Never my right, always my left. That's apparently where my censor sits. She has been in residence on my left shoulder for so many years that it's a wonder I'm not completely lopsided.

Here are some of the things she whispers, or shouts, depending on her mood, whenever I'm beginning something new:

This is stupid.

What a waste of time.

(Condescending laugh)

You really think you can pull that off?

So-and-so did it better.

What a dumb idea.

How boring.

Are you ready for a nap?

My inner censor wants to shut me down. She wants me to close up shop, like the man in one of my favorite *New Yorker* cartoons, who stands in the left frame, staring out a window looking bored, resigned. This frame is titled "Writer's Block: Temporary." The right frame shows him standing in the exact same way; nothing has changed, except now he's in front of a fish store bearing his name. The title? "Writer's Block: Permanent." My censor wants no less than to turn me into a fish salesman. Not that there's anything wrong with selling fish, except that I don't know anything about selling fish and am not particularly fond of the way it smells. What I do know--what I've spent the past couple of decades learning about myself—is that if I'm not writing, I'm not well. If I'm not writing, the world around me is slowly leached of its color. My senses are dulled. I am crabby with my husband, short-tempered with my kid, and more inclined to see small things wrong with my house (the crack in the ceiling, the smudge prints along the staircase wall) than look out the window at the blazing maple tree, the family of geese making its way across our driveway. If I'm not writing, my heart hardens, rather than lifts.

And so I have learned how to live with my censor. It doesn't happen by fighting her. It happens first by recognizing her— *oh, hello, it's you again*—and accepting our coexistence. Like those bumper stickers most often seen on the backs of Priuses spelling out *coexist* in the symbols of all the world's religions, the writer and her inner censor need to learn to get along. The I.C., once you're on a nickname basis, should be treated like an annoying, potentially undermining colleague. Try managing her with corporate-speak: *Thanks for reaching out, but can I circle back to you later?*

The daily discipline of this creates a muscle memory. It becomes ingrained, thereby habit. I try to remember this, each morning, as I make the solitary trek from the kitchen to my desk. My house is quiet. My family is gone. The hours stretch ahead of me. The beds have been made, the dogs have been walked. There is nothing stopping me. Nothing, except for the toxic little troll sitting on my left shoulder. Just when I think I have her beat, she will assume a new disguise. I have to be vigilant, on the ready. She will pretend to be well-intentioned. She's telling me *for my own good*.

Maybe you should try writing something more commercial.

You know, thrillers are hot. Why not write a thriller? Or at least a mystery?

Sweetheart (I hate it when she calls me sweetheart) no one wants to read a book about a depressed old man. Or a passive-aggressive mother. Why not write a book with a strong female protagonist, for a change? You know, a superheroine. Someone less . . . I don't know . . . victimy?

Under the guise of being helpful, or honest, my censor is like a guided missile aiming at every nook and cranny where I am at my weakest and most vulnerable. She will stoop and connive. All she wants to do is stop me from entering that sacred space from which the work springs. She is at her most insidious when I am at the beginning, because she knows that once I have begun, she will lose her power over me. And so I dip my toe into the stream. I feel the rush of words there. Words that are like a thousand silvery minnows, below the surface, rushing by. If I don't capture them, they will be lost.

CORNER

Start small. If you try to think about all of it at once—the world you hope to capture on the page, everything you know, every idea you've ever had, each person you've met, and the panoply of feelings coursing through you like a river—you'll be overcome with paralysis. Who wouldn't be? Just the way we put one foot in front of the other as we get out of bed, the way we brush our teeth, splash water on our faces, feed our animals if we have animals, and our children if we have them, measure the coffee, put on the kettle, we need to approach our writing one step at a time. It's impossible to evoke an entire world at the start. But it *is* possible to describe a crack in the sidewalk, the scuffed heel of a shoe. And that sidewalk crack or scuffed heel can be the point of entry, like a pinhole of light, to a story, a character, a universe.

Think of a jigsaw puzzle—one of those vexingly complicated puzzles that comes in a big box. Almost every family rec room has, at one point or another, seen one of these puzzles, spilled from its box, hundreds of pieces strewn across the floor. It starts out as a fun rainy day activity and—unless the family members are both freakishly patient and spacially gifted—there it will stay, gathering dust until, finally, someone sweeps all the puzzle pieces back into the box and retires it to the far reaches of a cupboard, never to be seen again. Too many colors and shapes! Too many possibilities! Where to even begin?

This is the writer's mind when embarking on a piece of work. We sit perched in front of our laptop screen, or our spiral-bound notebook, or giant desktop monitor, and—we freeze. After all, it's so important, isn't it, where we start? Don't we need a plan? Hadn't we better know where we're going? The stakes feel impossibly high. We're convinced that first word will dictate every word that follows. We are tyrannized by our options. All sorts of voices scream in our heads. First person or third? Present tense or past? The span of five minutes? Or two hundred years? What the hell are we doing? We don't know.

Build a corner. This is what people who are good at puzzles do. They ignore the heap of colors and shapes and simply look for straight edges. They focus on piecing together one tiny corner. Every book, story, and essay begins with a single word. Then a sentence. Then a paragraph. These words, sentences, paragraphs may well end up not being the actual beginning. You can't know that now. Straining to know the whole of the story before you set out is a bit like imagining great-grandchildren on a first date. But you can start with the smallest detail. Give us the gravel scattering along the highway as the pickup truck roars past. The crumb of food the wife wipes from her husband's beard. The ripped bottom of a girl's faded jeans. Anchor yourself somewhere—anywhere—on the page. You are committing, yes—but the commitment is to this tiny corner. One word. One image. One detail. Go ahead. Then see what happens next.

A Short Bad Book

One of my dearest friends began her last novel—one that went on to become a prizewinning best-seller—by telling herself that she was going to write a short, bad book. For a long time, she talked about the short, bad book she was writing. And she believed it. It released her from her fear of failure. It's a beautiful strategy. Anyone can write a short, bad book, right?

A while back, I was looking through a file on my computer in which I keep drafts of all my essays and stories and book reviews, and I realized that each one of these dozens of pieces had begun with the same phrase rolling through my head: *here goes nothing*. It's my version of telling myself that I'm going to write a short, bad book. *Here goes nothing*. The more we have at stake, the harder it is to make the leap into writing. The more we think about who's going to read it, what they're going to think, how many copies will be printed, whether this magazine or that magazine will accept it for publication, the further away we are from accomplishing anything alive on the page.

My son Jacob is in a rock band. When he starts learning a new song, he likes to spend a lot of time printing out the sheet music, getting it to look just right before he puts it in his binder. Then, he thinks about the YouTube video he wants to make, the record label who will sign them. All this, before he's learned to play the thing. I know this feeling well, this fantasy, these dreams of glory. I smile at them in my son, who, after all, is twelve and doing exactly what twelve-year-olds should be doing: trying on different identities for size. But I try to eliminate them in myself.

Years ago, I received my first big assignment from *The New Yorker*. On the checklist of dreams I pretended not to have, this was at the top. Now I had the chance. I had a contract for one of those "Personal History" pieces. A deadline. The story, which was an investigation into a family secret—an early, tragic marriage of my late father—was rich and sad and beautiful, and I wanted to do it justice. In the days and weeks after landing the assignment, I sat down each morning to write, and nothing happened. As I sat at my desk on West Ninety-second Street in Manhattan, instead of making the journalistic and imaginative leap into the world of Brooklyn circa 1948, I pictured my story in the pages of *The New Yorker*. What would it look like in *New Yorker* font? Would it have an illustration? What would the illustration be? Maybe they'd want an old picture of my dad. I made sure I had several of these around, should the photo department call.

I couldn't write. I grew tense. I was strangled by my own ego, by my petty desire for what I perceived to be the literary brass ring. I was missing the point, of course. The reward is in the doing. Most published writers will tell you that the moment they hold the book, or the prestigious magazine piece, or the good review, or the *whatever* in their hands—that moment is curiously hollow. It can't live up to the sweat, the solitude, the bloody battle that it represents.

I did eventually tire of my fantasies of being published in *The New Yorker,* and just got down to work. I set my alarm clock for a predawn hour and stumbled straight from bed to desk in an attempt to short-circuit the cocktail party chatter in my head, which went something like: *Oh, did you read . . . Yes, brilliant . . . and a National Magazine Award to boot,* and started with one word, and then another, then another, until I had a sentence. *Here goes nothing.* Eventually, I had pages. They were imperfect, maybe even *bad,* but I had begun. And these years later, when I think of that essay, what I remember most is not the moment I saw my work in *New Yorker* font, not when I saw the illustration of my father, not the congratulatory phone calls and notes that followed, but that predawn morning in my bedroom, at my desk, the lights of cars below on Broadway, my computer screen glowing in the dark.

A ROOM OF ONE'S OWN

It doesn't really matter what or where it is, as long as it is yours. I don't necessarily mean that it has to belong to you. Only that, for the time that you're working, you have what you need. Learning what you need to do your best work is a big step forward in the life of any writer. We all have different requirements, different ways of working. I have a friend who likes to write on the subway. She will board the F train just to get work done. The jostle and cacophony—she finds it clears her mind. Me? You'd have to shoot me first. For one, I'm a wee bit claustrophobic. Also, I need solitude and silence. I have friends who work best in coffee shops, others who like to work in the same room as their partners. Friends who have written multiple books at their kitchen tables. Marcel Proust famously wrote in bed, and so did Wendy Wasserstein. Gay Talese, the son of an Italian tailor, dresses in a custom-made suit each morning and descends the stairs to his basement study. Hemingway wrote standing up. One writer I know works best late at night, a habit left over from the years when she had young children under her roof and those were the only hours that were hers alone.

As I write these words, I am sitting in a small chair upholstered in a blue-and-white checkered pattern, my feet resting on an ottoman. I am in a guest bedroom in a large and empty house that belongs to a friend. My own home just a few miles away is uninhabitable because of a freak autumn blizzard that caused a loss of power all over New England. For the past couple of days I have burrowed into this chair and haven't moved for hours. I learned to make myself a cappuccino—caffeine being one of my requirements—using my friend's machine. I've worked well in this blue-and-white checkered chair. In this strange time-out-of-time, while my son has been sledding with friends and my husband has been driving around helping marooned motorists, I have been here in the silence, save for the hum of the generator. No one knows where I am. The Internet is down. The phone won't ring. There is no laundry to do, no rearranging of the spice drawer. And so this guest room in a borrowed home has become my room of my own.

We writers spend our days making something out of nothing. There is the blank page (or screen) and then there is the fraught and magical process of putting words down on that page. There is no shape, no blueprint until one emerges from the page, as if through a mist. Is it a mirage? Is it real? We can't know. And so we need a sense of structure around us. These four walls. This cup. The wheels of the train beneath us. This borrowed room. The weight of this particular pen. Whatever it is that makes us feel secure in our physical space allows us to make the leap, hoping that the page will catch us. Writing, after all, is an act of faith. We must believe, without the slightest evidence that believing will get us anywhere.

Recently I was wandering through one of my favorite stores in a town near my home, and I saw a chaise longue. It wasn't just any chaise longue, it was the perfect chaise longue, the one I had been dreaming of, the one I hadn't even known existed. Delicate yet sturdy, covered in an antique Tibetan blanket . . . oh, how I wanted it. It wasn't cheap, and I'm not in the habit of buying furniture on impulse, or really at all. I took a photo of the chaise with my phone, and occasionally, in the days that followed, I'd sneak a peek. I went back to the store often enough that the saleswoman asked me if I was coming to visit my chair. Finally, I plunked down my credit card, feeling slightly sick to my stomach. There are a lot of things we need in our home more than a chaise longue covered by an antique Tibetan blanket. A generator, for instance. But I had to have it, and here's why: although I have an office in my home, it had grown stale. My desk was piled high with papers, mail, and various forms that had nothing to do with my writing life. My office had begun to feel like a prison rather than a sanctuary. It's walls no longer supported me and the view out my window might as well have been of a brick wall rather than a lovely meadow. I needed a change. I knew I would write well, that I would curl up and *read* well, in that chaise longue. I would settle myself on that soft Tibetan blanket, my notebook in my lap, books strewn all around me. Safe and secure in that space, I'd dare to dig for the elusive words.

In my yoga practice, I have been taught to begin in mountain pose. Mountain pose—standing with feet slightly apart, with head, neck, and pelvis in alignment, eyes softly focused, face relaxed—is a grounding pose. Until we can feel the ground beneath our feet, supporting us, we cannot attempt the other poses: eagle, dancer, warrior. We need to be rooted before we can fly. And although those other poses might look more challenging, sometimes it feels as if mountain pose is the most challenging of all. To be still. To be grounded. To claim one's place in the world.

TRACTION

In our New Jersey neighborhood when I was young, a family called the Adlers lived a few blocks away. If you can have a crush not just on one person but on an entire family, I had one on the Adlers. The father, mother, two sons and daughter seemed to be everything my small family was not. Their house was alive with comings and goings. Cars and bicycles filled their driveway. They always had visitors for weekend lunch, and dined outdoors in warm weather, the sound of their easy conversation drifting through the hedges that separated their backyard from the street. They were content with each other— a family who sought out the company only of itself.

Most Sundays, I would ride my bike in circles around their block until one of them would notice me and wave me over. The kids were all older than me, and they took me in, sort of the way you'd take in a cute but needy stray cat. I was twelve, thirteen, fourteen years old, and they would gently tease me. Harvey and Eddie Adler would tell me that they'd wait for me and marry me some day. They were both in medical school, and on weekends they'd bring home girlfriends—beautiful, sophisticated, long-haired young women who wore stacked-heel boots and dangling earrings, who were in law school or did social work or advertising. I wanted to be them. I wanted to skip my teenage years entirely and leapfrog into adulthood. I wanted out of my parents' quiet house and the feeling I couldn't shake that something was very wrong.

Sorrow had by then taken up a permanent place in our home. My father injured his back and underwent spinal-fusion surgery, which at the time was quite dangerous. Now I understand the chronic pain that would have driven a man to sign up for an operation that carried with it a real risk of paralysis. But back then, I watched my father fade into an angry, rigid, stricken figure who hung in traction from the door of our den, the folds of his neck squished around his face by a brace, watching *Hogan's Heroes*. I didn't know about the failures, both real and self-perceived, that had become too much for him to bear. I didn't know about the Valium and codeine that he had begun to abuse. I didn't know anything about my parents' marriage except that a brittleness existed between them, the air so dry that it seemed always ready to ignite.

It would be twenty more years before I would get the assignment from *The New Yorker* and, through the writing of it, begin to understand. I exhumed the ghost of my father's early marriage to a young woman who was dying of non-Hodgkin's lymphoma as she walked down the aisle. A woman whose name had never been uttered in our home but who was later described to me, by relatives and friends I interviewed, as the love of his life. As a writer, I assembled and arranged the pieces of my grieving young father on the page until they became a portrait—true to memory, reporting, imagination. A collage and an elegy.

All I knew then, with the canny survival instincts of a teenager, was that the Adler house was way more fun than ours. Harvey and Eddie played tennis with me, and on another neighbor's court I became a strong player, slamming the ball boy-style, low over the net, but mostly I was eyeing Eddie's thighs, his blond hair glistening in the sun. That tennis court, those young medical students, their noblesse oblige willingness to call me into their midst—those were the hours in which it seemed a door opened to a brighter, easier, happier future. Who knew? Maybe Eddie *would* wait for me.

The year I turned sixteen, the youngest Adler, a dark, wild beauty named Joyce, was found lying unconscious on the floor of her college dormitory room. She'd had a stroke—a freak aneurysm—from which she never recovered. She and I hadn't been close—I was an interloper, she tolerated me—but I had admired and envied her for what I imagined to be her perfect life. The first time I went to visit her, at a rehabilitation center in New Jersey, she was propped in a wheelchair, her eyes unfocused, her face contorted. She remained quadriplegic and unable to speak, but fully conscious, for the next twenty years until she died. This was my awakening. *Randomness, suddenness, the fickle nature of good fortune.* These drilled themselves into me, and eventually became the themes central to all of my work. I started sleeping with Eddie Adler when I was seventeen, and he very quickly broke my heart. *Things are not what they seem.* The Adler parents were never again able to look at me without thinking: *Why not you?* My father, pale and wincing in pain. A lazy Susan in the center of our kitchen table, slowly filling with narcotics. My mother, who hadn't paid attention to her wedding vows. *For better or for worse.*

From the chaise longue, the subway seat, the borrowed room, we see: a man hanging in traction, his angry wife, the strong, tanned thighs of a callow medical student, a beautiful, ruined girl. We see: a still and silent house, a bicycle circling, a girl who is lost, who is confused by all she sees, for which she doesn't have language. She will grow up to find the language. Finding the language. It's what we can hope for.

SHIMMER

Ann Sexton once remarked in an interview, when asked why she wrote such dark and painful poems, that pain engraves a deeper memory. *Pain engraves a deeper memory.* Think of a time in your own life when you have experienced a sudden shock, a betrayal, terrible news. Perhaps you remember the weather, the quality of the breeze, a half-full ashtray, a scratch on the wooden floor, the moth-eaten sweater you were wearing, the siren in the distance. Pain carves details into us, yes. I would wager, though, that great joy does as well. Strong emotion, Virginia Woolf said, must leave its trace. Start writing, grow still and quiet, press toward that strong emotion and you will discover it anew. The Adlers were the first of a particular kind of hurt for me. And so they stayed alive inside of me. They are alive still.

These traces that live within us often lead us to our stories. Joan Didion called this a *shimmer around the edges*. Emerson called it a gleam. "A man should learn to detect and watch that gleam of light which flashes across his mind from within," he wrote in his great essay, "On Self Reliance." "Yet he dismisses without notice his thought, because it is his." *Because it is his.* That knowledge, that *ping,* the hair on our arms standing up, that sudden, electric sense of knowing. We must learn to watch for these moments. To not discount them. To take note: *I'll have to write about this.* It can happen in a split second, or as a slow dawning. It happens when our histories collide with the present. When it arrives, it's unmistakable, indelible. It comes with the certainty of its own rightness. When I first met my husband, at a Halloween party, I thought: *There you are.* It's a bit like that with our subject matter. We don't walk around trolling for ideas like people on beaches with those funny little machines, panning for coins; we don't go looking on the equivalent of match.com in search of Emerson's gleam. But when we stumble upon it, we know. We know because it shimmers. And if you are a writer, you will find that you won't give up that shimmer for anything. You live for it. Like falling in love, moments that announce themselves as your subject are rare, and there's a magic to them. Ignore them at your own peril.

Permission

If you're waiting for the green light, the go-ahead, the reassuring wand to tap your shoulder and anoint you as a writer, you'd better pull out your thermos and folding chair because you're going to be waiting for a good long while. Accountants go to business school and when they graduate with their degrees, they don't ask themselves whether they have permission to do people's taxes. Lawyers pass the bar, medical students become doctors, academics become professors, all without considering whether or not they have a right to be going to work. But nothing and no one gives us permission to wake up and sit at home staring at a computer screen while everybody else sets their alarm clocks, puts on reasonable attire, and boards the train. No one is counting on us, or waiting for whatever we produce. People look at us funny, very possibly because we look funny, strange, and out of sync with the rest of the world after spending our days alone in our bathrobes, talking only to our household pets, if at all. I can't imagine what my UPS delivery guy thinks when I crack open the door to sign for a package. *There's that weird lady again.* My husband, who has been a successful journalist and screenwriter for most of his adult life, was in his forties before his father stopped asking him when he was going to get a real job.

Sure, there are advanced degrees in writing and various signifiers that a career might be under way, but ultimately a writer is someone who writes. And a writer who writes is one who finds a way to give herself permission. The advanced degree is useless in this regard. No writer I know wakes up in the morning and, while brushing her teeth, thinks: *Check me out, I have an MFA.* Or, for that matter, *I've published x number of books,* or even, *I've won the Pulitzer Prize.* There is no magical place of arrival. There is only the solitary self facing the page.

It's strange and challenging, glorious and devastating, this business of being a writer. Every day, a new indignity. The rejection is without end. Almost any short story you ever see published in *The Atlantic Monthly* or *Harper's* has been rejected first by *The New Yorker.* Press many of us—including those you'd think might have moved beyond this—and you will discover that we can quote you the most painful passages from our worst reviews. We can give you a list of critics who are dismissive of our work. We'll tell you which judge on what academic committee blackballed us. On some mornings, these rejections, reviews, enemies seem to stand between us and our work like a mutant army. *Who are you to give yourself permission to write?* They seem to shout. We writers are a thin-skinned, anxious lot, and often feel like we're getting away with something, that we're going to be revealed, at any moment, as the frauds we really are.

Whether you are a writer just mustering up the nerve to sign up for your first weekend workshop, or filling out your MFA applications, or one gazing moodily out from a big poster in the window of your local Barnes & Noble, you are far from alone in this business of granting yourself the permission to do your work. Masters of the form quake before the page. They often feel hopeless and despairing. They may also fall prey to petty musings. They have days in which they simply can't get out of their own way.

But when we give ourselves permission, we move past this. The world once again reveals itself to us. We become open and aware, patient and ready to receive it. We don't ask why that particular slant of sunlight, snippet of dialogue, old couple walking along the road hand-in-hand seems to evoke an entire world. We give ourselves permission because we are the only ones who can do so. There's a great expression in Twelve Step programs: *Act as if.* Act as if you're a writer. Sit down and begin. Act as if you might just create something beautiful, and by beautiful I mean something authentic and universal. Don't wait for anybody to tell you it's okay. Take that shimmer and show us our humanity. That's your job.

READING

On my desk, propped between two Buddha-head bookends, are my most essential books. Virginia Woolf's *A Writer's Diary,* and Thomas Merton's *Thoughts In Solitude* are always in this small grouping. For several years, I kept Ian McEwan's *Saturday* and Alice Munro's *Runaway* close by as well, because they were two contemporary works that, when I read them back-to-back, unlocked the mystery of close third person narration. Right now, in a pile next to my chaise longue, are this year's editions of *The Best American Short Stories* and *The Best American Essays,* just so I always have something to dip into.

When I meet someone who wants to be a writer, and yet doesn't read much, I wonder how that works. What would provide you with nourishment, with inspiration? I'm focused on my own writing, students sometimes say. I don't have time to read. Or they tell me they're afraid of being influenced, as if they might catch the voice of another writer like a virulent strain of flu. But reading good prose *is* influence. When my son was little, he used to imitate Johnny Damon's batting stance, or Roger Federer's topspin forehand. In this way, he began to learn how to play. When we follow the intricate loops of a Pynchon sentence, or pause in the white-space minimalism of Carver, we are seeing what is possible, and we bring that sense of possibility to the page.

Reading is also camaraderie. It is a challenge, a balm, a beacon. "Who would call a day spent reading a good day?" asks Annie Dillard. "But a life spent reading—that is a good life." I try (most of the time I fail, but still, I try) to begin my day reading. And by this I do not mean *The New York Times* online, or the *Vanity Fair* lying on the kitchen table, or the e-mails that have accumulated overnight, and which I open at my own risk. The roulette of the in-box! An enticing invitation to a private online sale of gourmet Himalayan sea salt, a high school nemesis emerging from the ether—whatever it is, it's the opposite of reading. It pulls you away, instead of directing you inward.

Fill your ears with the music of good sentences, and when you finally approach the page yourself, that music will carry you. It will remind you that you are a part of a vast symphony of writers, that you are not alone in your quest to lay down words, each one bumping against the next until something new is revealed. It will exhort you to do better. To not settle for just good enough. Reading great work is exhilarating. It shows us what's possible. When I start the morning with any one of the dozens of books in rotation on my office floor, my day is made instantly better, brighter. I never regret having done it. Think about it: have you ever spent an hour reading a good book, and then had that sinking, queasy feeling of having wasted time?

TOEHOLD

For some writers, it's a character. For others, it's place. And for still others, it's plot, or a snippet of dialogue. What's our way into the story? When do we have enough to begin? If we're climbing a mountain, we need something to grab on to. We wedge our foot into a crevice in the rock and pull ourselves up. We are feeling our way in the dark.

We have nothing to go by, but still, we must begin. It requires chutzpah—the Yiddish word for that ineffable combination of courage and hubris—to put down one word, then another, perhaps even accumulate a couple of flimsy pages, so few that they don't even form the smallest of piles, and call it the beginning of a novel. Or memoir. Or story. Or anything, really, other than a couple of flimsy pages.

When I'm between books, I feel as if I will never have another story to tell. The last book has wiped me out, has taken everything from me, everything I understand and feel and know and remember, and . . . that's it. There's nothing left. A low-level depression sets in. The world hides its gifts from me. It has taken me years to realize that this feeling, the one of the well being empty, is as it should be. It means I've spent everything. And so I must begin again.

I wait.

I try to be patient. I remember Colette, who wrote that her most essential art was "not that of writing, but the domestic task of knowing how to wait, to conceal, to save up crumbs, to reglue, regild, change the worst into the not-so-bad, how to lose and recover in the same moment that frivolous thing, a taste for life." Colette's words, along with those of a few others, have migrated from one of my notebooks to another for over twenty years now. It's wisdom I need to remember—wisdom that is so easy to forget.

A number of years ago, I was in the midst of this waiting, and was growing impatient, despondent. This time, I was convinced, was different. This time, I really had nothing. The well was never going to fill up again. This kind of thinking usually leads me to ruminate about applying to medical school, and then I rapidly come to the conclusion that I'm too old, and can't even help my son with sixth grade math. I had the faintest hint of a new idea, but it was not something that felt alive inside of me. I felt no spark, saw no shimmer. The idea—and I knew enough to beware of free-floating ideas—had to do with a daughter who was estranged from her mother. The mother still lived in the small rural town, in the same house where the daughter had been raised, and now she was dying, so the daughter was forced to return to the place of her childhood.

Yeah, I know. Sounds sort of familiar, doesn't it? A variation on a theme of books we've all read. The daughter wasn't clear to me. The town was abstract, and I didn't even feel like writing a novel set in a small town. I had just done that. I had no sense of the nature of the estrangement. I went on like this for months—doing nothing, until one day, I was driving to New York City with my husband. It's nearly a two-hour drive from our house to the city, one which we do often. Michael was driving and I was looking out the window at the blur of the familiar landscape, when suddenly the entire novel came to me in a rush.

The story didn't take place in a small town, I realized. The mother lived in Manhattan, on the Upper West Side. In fact, she lived in the Apthorp, a building at Seventy-ninth Street and Broadway. On the twelfth floor. In a rent-stabilized apartment that she had bought when the building went condo. Her name was Ruth Dunne. She was a famous photographer who had taken provocative photographs of her daughter as a child. For years, I had been fascinated by Sally Mann, well-known for a series of controversial photographs of her children. I had wondered what had happened to the children, particularly the oldest daughter—what must it have been like to be her mother's muse?—but Sally Mann had never shimmered for me before, nor had the Apthorp, a building I had walked by countless times. But suddenly, here it all was. The mother, the daughter, the estrangement.

That was it. I had it—the toehold—my way to begin climbing the mountain. My novel, *Black & White,* presented itself to me during that car ride as if it had been waiting behind a curtain. Why that particular car ride on that particular day? Who knows. The easy silence between my husband and me. The familiar route. The overcast sky. It was the first time in my writing life that *place* had come first in defining a new piece of work. The moment I understood that the action took place in the Apthorp, the characters began to reveal themselves to me. Your way in will not always be the same. There are no rules, and you cannot force it, but you can show up every day and practice the art of waiting.

SEEDS

Once, while visiting Los Angeles, a friend urged me to see her healer. She wouldn't tell me anything about how this healer practiced his craft. "Trust me. Just go," she said. So I made an appointment. My friend was a walking advertisement for the healer; she was radiant, joyful. I was not, nor had I ever been, joyful. I had moments of contentment, but euphoria wasn't in my emotional range. I parked my car in front of a bungalow, then pulled open a painted wooden gate and walked through lush gardens to a converted garage in back, where the healer—a tall man with flowing gray hair and lively blue eyes—explained to me that he would be plucking out the seeds of childhood sorrow and pain, so that they would no longer be sprouting tangled weeds in my adult life.

I sat opposite him on a sofa, and answered a series of questions.

Parents?

Dead.

Children?

One.

Married?

Happily.

After a little while, the healer came over to me and placed a hand on my solar plexus. "You have many beings inside of you," he said. "Are you ready to release them?"

I nodded, though I felt as if I was acting in a play. I focused on a painting of the Buddha sitting in a field of psychedelic flowers. The healer made slow circles just below my rib cage.

"What was your mother like?"

"Difficult."

"And your father?"

"Kind."

"Your mother's mother? Were you close?"

"Not particularly."

"What did you call her?"

"Grammy."

The circles got faster. The healer instructed me to lean forward and exhale forcefully, three times. And again. "There," he said, his gaze trailing away, as if watching someone leave. "Now repeat after me: Go to the light, Grammy."

"Go to the light, Grammy."

My own voice rang in my ears.

"Again."

"Go to the light, Grammy."

The process was repeated for my mother, my father, several aunts and uncles, and finally the healer asked if I'd had any childhood pets.

"A dog."

"What kind?"

"He was a poodle."

"Name?"

Here I hesitated, embarrassed. It wasn't even a name I had made up. I copied our neighbors, who had named their poodle first.

"Poofy," I reluctantly answered.

"And you loved Poofy," the healer said.

Honestly, I didn't remember feeling very fond of Poofy. He was a bit short on personality. But I reached back in my memory for that small body, that curly black bundle.

"Good," the healer said. He seemed to be watching Poofy trot out the door along with Grammy. "Now tell him it's okay to go."

"Go to the light, Poofy," I said. "Poofy, go to the light."

At the end of the hour-long session, my solar plexus was sore from all the rubbing, but I didn't feel much else. My friend had promised that I'd feel changed, transformed. That I'd feel an infinite ease. Instead, I felt silly and a little sad. As I drove the streets of Los Angeles, I thought about my parents, my grandmother, aunts, uncles, and even Poofy. Did I want them to leave me? Did I want them to go to the light? The healer had talked about seeds. Even if those seeds could be plucked—the healer had made a pincer out of two fingers and pulled through the air—it seemed to me that they were important, and that getting rid of them might not be a good idea at all.

Who are we without everything that's ever happened to us? And if we are writers, how can we do our work without the grounding of our own history? Flannery O'Connor once wrote that anyone who has survived his childhood has enough material to last a lifetime. Those seeds are the material. When

I am writing, when it's going well, I have traveled to the place inside of me where I can locate them. They're very small, and not always easy to find. The way my grandmother said my full name, emphasizing the first syllable. *Dan*-eile. The crinkle of newspaper beneath Poofy's feet in the kitchen. My father's favorite piece of music: Dvorak's *New World Symphony*. The shortcut through the woods to school, the canopy of trees. These are words, phrases, faces, animals, street corners, strains of music that I need to hold on to, even if they sprout tangled weeds, even if remembering them causes the sadness and inevitable pain of loss. They contain within them the whole world.

THE BLANK PAGE

Michelangelo saw a statue in every block of marble, "shaped and perfect in attitude and action"—an angel waiting to be released. The woodworker George Nakashima believed that when a true craftsman brought out the grain that had been imprisoned in the trunk of a tree, he "found God within." I've long envied those artists who work with materials such as these—clay, marble, granite, wood—because I imagine the feeling is one of collaboration. The material itself contains the shape, the solution. It imposes limits, parameters. If the artist looks and listens carefully, the answer will be revealed: an arm, a thigh, a pattern, an angle, the drape of a robe.

The blank page offers no such gifts. When we greet it, we are quite rightly filled with trepidation. *What are you?* we wonder. *What will you yield to us?* The page gazes impassively back. It will give us nothing. It will take everything. It isn't interested in how we think or what we feel. It doesn't care if we fill it with words, or if we crumple it up in despair.

Once, I took an assignment from a newspaper to write something called "Tag Team Fiction." The idea was to pair two writers to do a story together. One would begin; the other would take up where the story left off; then—tag, you're it!— back and forth it would go until the story was completed. I was paired with a friend, the writer Meg Wolitzer. I don't remember which of us began, but I remember the feeling of waking up in the morning and opening my computer to see that my story had magically grown overnight. I had gone to sleep and it had written itself! And it was pretty good, too. Back and forth we went, in a dance, a duet, a writer's fantasy, which was that the pages seemed to be accumulating on their own, as we slept, or did errands, or went to the gym.

Aside from that one wacky assignment, I've never again had the experience of the page giving me anything that I hadn't put there all by myself. See, the thing is this: *you can't know.* You can't know if it's going to work. You can't know if it's good, or has the potential to be good. You can spend days, weeks, *years,* working on something that you will end up throwing away, or, in the more gentle way of phrasing it, putting it in a drawer. It's a lot like the rest of life, in that way. We want to know. Will this relationship work out? Will our children be successful and happy? Will this risk pay off? We fall in love, we have babies, we take risks. The alternative is cowardice. We show up—for life, for writing. We act like brave people, even when we don't feel like brave people. And so we begin to lay down the words. We fill the page with them. Michelangelo had his marvelous hunks of marble, Nakashima communed with the interiors of trees, and we have this. We are in mid-dive and the words are the water below.

Don't think too much. There'll be time to think later. Analysis won't help. You're chiseling now. You're passing your hands over the wood. Now the page is no longer blank. There's something there. It isn't your business yet to know whether it's going to be prize-worthy someday, or whether it will gather dust in a drawer. Now you've carved the tree. You've chiseled the marble. You've begun.

OUTSIDER

My mother was my father's third wife. My father was my mother's second husband. My mother was forty and my father was forty-two when I was born. Today, preschool halls are filled with gray-haired parents in their forties and fifties—parents who've lived whole other lives before their children were born. But back then, this made my parents different. It also made them stay married over many years of a contentious relationship. They each saw themselves as having failed before, and those perceived failures bound them together.

My father was the scion of a deeply religious Jewish family. My mother was not a believer, though she went along for the ride. She was fun-loving, glamorous, and wanted to wear a beautiful dress and be the belle of the ball. He was quiet, introspective, thoughtful; she twirled around the room, singing, arms flung wide. They fought. Oh, how they fought—endlessly, bitterly, in harsh whispers. They disagreed on most things, but the single source of their greatest conflict was me.

Until I was twelve, I was sent to a religious day school where I spent half the day learning in Hebrew, and the other half in English. At thirteen, my mother presumably having worn my father down, I began to attend a local prep school where both Jews and girls were a new phenomenon. But my awareness of myself as an outsider was in full flower long before this. When two people who shouldn't be married to each other bring a child into the world, that child—I'm distancing myself here, making myself into a character—*that child* cannot help but feel as if she's navigating the world on a borrowed visa. Her papers aren't in order. Her right to be here is in question.

Whether at the yeshiva or the prep school, whether within the quiet walls of my family home or circling the neighborhood on my bike, wherever I went I felt like a foreign correspondent on the sidelines of my own life. I spent my days observing. I took note of the way Amy Stifel tilted her head to the side when she laughed; the faded rectangle on the back pocket of Kathy Kimber's jeans that was the exact shape and size of a pack of cigarettes; the fact that the Spanish teacher always looked like she had just stopped crying. At home, I studied my parents. My mother's posture was ramrod straight, her jaw lifted, her mouth curved into a small smile as if at any moment a camera might be pointed in her direction. My father seemed to slump as my mother grew taller. He gained weight, his belly straining over his belt. She started making more trips into New York City, where she took art classes, saw a therapist. His prescription bottles took over the kitchen counter, replacing garlic tablets and Vitamin E supplements.

Some Day This Pain Will be Useful to You is the title of my friend Peter Cameron's novel. Looking back now, from my writing study on the second floor of my home on a hill, I see a stone wall, the bare branches of a white birch tree. I see climbing wisteria on the split wood shingles of our roof. It's a school holiday, and my husband and son are out to breakfast at a nearby diner. The dogs pad around in the next room. A cappuccino in a small ceramic mug brought back from a trip to Italy has grown cold by my side. It's a day. A day full of writing, reading, thinking, driving, of a child's piano lesson, a holiday party later on. A day that holds me, connects me to the spinning world.

So the pain did indeed turn out to be useful—but only later, much later. At the time, it was more complicated than I had tools for. I worried that my parents would get a divorce. Sometimes I worried that they *wouldn't* get a divorce. I regularly imagined that my father would die. Never my mother, only my father. A series of images ran through my mind like a looping reel of film: my father, clutching at his chest, falling over on the sidewalk. My father, collapsing on his way to synagogue. When I wasn't preoccupied with my father's death, I thought about my own. I was certain that I would die very young. That something was already wrong with me. I poked and prodded at my body. Was that a lump on my thigh, or a mosquito bite? Every headache was a brain tumor. Maybe I would just disappear.

I endured these fantasies and premonitions by writing about them. The stories I made up were medicinal. My inner life was barbed, with jagged edges. Left untended, it felt dangerous, like it might turn on me at any moment. Intuitively, I understood that I had to *use* it. It was all I had. By writing, I was participating in a tradition as old as humanity. *I was here.* Hieroglyphs on rock. *I was here, and this is my story.*

HABIT

People sometimes ask if I write every day. They're incredulous when I answer that I write five days a week, Monday through Friday, and keep as close to banker's hours as I can manage. They tell me that they can't imagine it. They'd get lonely. Or distracted. Or bored. They need more stimulation. The track of this particular conversation often ends up with the person telling me that they'll write a book when they retire, or hire someone to ghostwrite their life story.

You must be so *disciplined,* they say.

And I stand there with a smile frozen in place, not wanting to be rude, but not knowing how to respond.

It's my *job,* I want to say. It has nothing to do with discipline.

But where do you find the *inspiration?* they'll ask.

I sit down every day at around the same time and put myself in the path of inspiration, I sometimes say, if the person seems genuinely interested. If I don't sit down, if I'm not there working, then inspiration will pass right by me, like the right guy in a romantic comedy who's on the other side of the party but the girl never sees because she's focused on her total loser of a date.

It's hard to overestimate the importance of habit. Of routine. I've had students who have full-time jobs—one who comes to mind is a psychologist and AIDS researcher and the mother of two young children, who wrote her first novel in the predawn hours. Another student, a book editor, worked on her first novel for precisely one uninterrupted hour before heading to her office job each day. So much can be accomplished in one focused hour, especially when that hour is part of a routine, a sacred rhythm that becomes part of your daily life.

In the yoga and meditation practices that have become integral to my writing day, I rarely feel like unrolling my mat. There's always something more pressing to do. Searching online for that perfect black leather jacket on sale, for instance. But I know that if I just begin the motions, the ritual, of setting up my practice, I will probably overcome the pull of high fashion, or whatever the day's distraction happens to be. If I light a fire in the fireplace, then the lavender-scented candle; if I get my music set up and unroll my mat; if I put the crystals on the floor that have become part of my routine, then the next thing I know, I'm in a sun salutation, and an hour goes by. I'm in lotus position, counting my breath. I haven't waited to be in the mood. I've just gone ahead and done it anyway, because that's what I've been doing for years now.

It's the same with writing, which is a practice like any other. If I waited to be in the mood to write, I'd barely have a chapbook of material to my name. Who would ever be in the mood to write? Do marathon runners get in the mood to run? Do teachers wake up with the urge to lecture? I don't know, but I doubt it. My guess is that it's the very act that is generative. The doing of the thing that makes possible the desire for it. A runner suits up, stretches, begins to run. An inventor trudges down to his workroom, closing the door behind him. A writer sits in her writing space, setting aside the time to be alone with her work. Is she inspired doing it? Very possibly not. Is she distracted, bored, lonely, in need of stimulation? Oh, absolutely, without a doubt it's hard to sit there. Who wants to sit there? Something nags at the edges of her mind. Should she make soup for dinner tonight? She's on the verge of jumping up from her chair—in which case all will be lost—but wait. Suddenly she remembers: this is her hour (or two, or three). This is her habit, her job, her discipline. Think of a ballet dancer at the barre. *Plié, elevé, battement tendu.* She is practicing, because she knows that there is no difference between practice and art. The practice *is* the art.

BIG IDEAS

If you're sitting down to begin something new, your fingers hovering over the keyboard, or pen poised in your hand like a maestro before a symphony orchestra, if you are thinking: *I'm going to write a story about race and class in the American South, told in two voices, and one voice will be in the first person, present tense, and the other will be in the third person, past tense, and I will explore themes of longing and regret, oppression and denial,* you're in trouble. These are ideas. They're the babbling of a writer in the delusional grip of a fantasy that she is in control.

I've learned to be wary of those times when I think I know what I'm doing. I've discovered that my best work comes from the uncomfortable but fruitful feeling of not having a clue—of being worried, secretly afraid, even convinced that I'm on the wrong track. When I think I know what I'm doing—when I have a big idea—I tend to start talking about it. First, I might bring it up to my husband: *I'm thinking of writing a novel that moves backward in time.* Or, having clipped a newspaper article, *I think there's a good story here about the juror who forced a mistrial.* Instead of sitting with a thought, I release my tension by blabbing about it. No good will come of this. The point is best made by Frederick Nietzsche: "That for which we find words is already dead in our hearts. There is always a kind of contempt in the act of speaking." I keep Nietzsche's words on an index card tacked to a bulletin board above my desk as a reminder, a warning, that it isn't usually useful to talk about or to over-think what you haven't yet written. After all, if we write out of the tension of the unexpressed, where does the tension go once we've expressed it?

Let go of every *should* or *shouldn't* running through your mind when you start. Be willing to stand at the base of a new mountain, and with humility and grace, bow to it. Allow yourself to understand that it's bigger than you, or anything you can possibly imagine. You're not sure of the path. You're not even sure where the next step will take you. When you begin, whisper to yourself: *I don't know.*

GETTING TO WORK

I have written seven books, and still I have to remind myself that this is what I do, this is my vocation, this is what puts food on the table and pays the mortgage. It's not a hobby, or something I spend my days doing for the sheer joy of it. It's not—as some people like to think, as if writers are home crafting cute animals out of Play-Doh—*so much fun!* If I had a regular job (or what my writer friends and I have long referred to as job-jobs), I'd have a boss. Maybe multiple bosses. There would be meetings, conference calls, expectations, a day shaped for me, rather than by me.

We writers shape our own days. We sit at our desks in our pajamas. We putter around empty houses, watering plants, making stews in the slow cooker, staring out the window, and we call it "working." We close our doors when our husbands or wives or kids are downstairs watching TV. *Shhh! I'm working!* And at the same time, often we don't have anything to show for it. We have no guarantee that what we're doing will amount to anything resembling art.

Every day, when I wake up, when my bare feet hit the cold wood of my bedroom floor and I begin the process— scrambling the eggs, pouring the juice, packing the sandwiches, locating sneakers, yelling "bye, drive carefully" as my husband and son head off—I try to remember that to sit down and write is a gift. That if I do not seize this day, it will be lost. I think of writers I admire who are no longer living. I'm aware that the simple fact of *being here* creates a kind of responsibility, even a moral one, to get to work.

AUDIENCE OF ONE

Who do we write for? Our friends, enemies, ex-lovers? Our families? The vast reading public? Ourselves? I find that the more people are in my head when I write, the less I am able to accomplish. It can get very busy in there. It can start to feel like a crowded subway during rush hour, no one meeting each other's eyes, just waiting for the doors to open. So I try to heed the advice of Kurt Vonnegut, who once said that he wrote for an audience of one.

This audience of one doesn't have to be a person you know. She doesn't even need to be alive and on the planet. Vonnegut wrote for his sister, who had died years earlier. It's not about sharing the work, but about creating a connection. The wire that stretches from writer to reader is singular. The writer creates in solitude, and the reader reads in solitude. Each is unknown to the other but, nonetheless, an intimate relationship is forged. We don't stop in the middle of *Madame Bovary* and think of all the other readers throughout history who have fallen under its spell, any more than we stop in the midst of lovemaking to think of the lovers who have come before us. Our absorption in a great book demands that we think only of ourselves and of the author to whom we are, at that moment, bound. We flip to the back inside flap and, if there is a photograph of the author, we examine it for clues. Are his eyes sad? Why is she looking away? What's behind that half-smile? And we imagine—whether consciously or not—that the author has been writing directly to us.

I write to one specific reader at a time. My audience of one, over the years, has changed. In the beginning, it was my dead father. I longed to reach out to him, through time and space, to have him know the woman I was becoming. Then, sometimes, it was my mother. Each sentence I wrote felt like a plea. *Please understand me.* Later, it became my husband—it still is. And now, my audience of one is also my son, in the hopes that someday, he will find his mother in the pages of her books.

SMITH CORONA

Behind the closed door to her office, my mother typed. Most nights, I fell asleep to the thunderous clacking of the keys on her Smith Corona, the high, thin *ding* of the carriage as she pushed the return lever at the end of each line. In her office—which shared a wall with my bedroom—she sat behind a big wooden desk piled with papers and boxes. She made carbon copies of everything she wrote. Not an inch of the surface of the desk was ever visible. If I close my eyes now, I can hear her. She was a very fast typist, with long, strong fingers. The steady rhythm—*tikatikatikatikatika, ding! tikatikatikatikatika, ding!*—was my childhood lullaby. In the sound of those keys, I heard frustration, anger, longing, determination, regret.

My mother was always starting things she didn't finish. Some of her ideas had nothing to do with writing, notably a line of jewelry for which she manufactured a prototype of a twenty-four-karat gold tennis ball pendant, with a sapphire in its center, the motto being *Keep your eye on the ball!* But her greatest efforts went into writing projects. One was a children's book called *Yes, Mary Ann, the World is Round,* a story about a girl whose dolls spring to life and tell her all about the countries they come from, for which my mother hired a famous children's photographer and used me as a model. I still have the manuscript for this book, the photographs encased in plastic sleeves: me as a five-year-old in a yellow flannel Lanz nightgown, holding my dolls.

My mother attempted most genres: children's books, poems, essays, journalism, and writing for TV, big screen, and stage. She wrote spec scripts for *The Partridge Family* and *Hawaii Five-O* and sent them in manila envelopes to the offices of the Hollywood producers whose names were listed in the shows' credits. She didn't know that submitting scripts in this manner was about as effective as making them into paper airplanes and flying them out the window. She had a strange, strained combination of cluelessness and desire. She flitted from project to project, never seeing anything through to the end.

I was highly attuned to my mother. I felt and sensed her moods the way an animal can feel thunder and lightning miles away. She was my first lesson in character and point of view. I watched her carefully. I always, *always* knew what she was thinking. The way she behaved and what she felt were often at odds. She might, for example, be dancing around the kitchen, singing *tra-la-la-la* in her wobbly soprano and conducting with a wooden spoon, but she was staving off some sort of darkness—a rejection, an insult, a slight.

Her most impassioned work was epistolary, and her Smith Corona was her weapon: she wrote letters to the mayor, the rabbi, the president of the United States. The letters were full of emphasis, as made clear by whole paragraphs in capitals, rows of exclamation points, sentences underlined in red pen or yellow highlighter, or sometimes both. My mother was filled with what seemed to be a bottomless ire. She was fueled by self-righteous indignation, which was only made worse when the mayor, the rabbi, and the president of the United States didn't personally write back.

Tikatikatikatikatika, ding! Tikatikatikatikatika, ding! A girl falls asleep each night to the song of a typewriter. A girl—once again I become a character in my own childhood—feels the unhappiness simmering beneath her mother's determination. The girl tries hard to please her mother. (Many years later, when she's a grown woman, one of her aunts will turn to her and say: "Do you want to make your mother happy? Do you really, really want to make your mother happy?" Oh, yes. Yes, she did. "Well, then move in with her," the aunt said.) And back then, the girl believed that her very survival depended on being good, and pretty, and accommodating, and all the things her mother wanted her to be. She had no way of knowing that it was a losing battle. That no matter what she did, she herself would someday be identified as the cause of her mother's misery. Eventually, she would be the recipient of long letters—carbon copies—covered with red ink and yellow highlighter and rows of exclamation points.

"How dare you?" Once I was a grown woman—a writer, a teacher of writing—this came to be one of my mother's favorite rants. "How dare you?" As I sit on my chaise longue covered by the antique Tibetan blanket, my dogs sleeping by my feet, the wind blowing hard outside my window, my small computer balanced on my lap, books and papers all around me, my mother gone eight years now, I can still hear her trembling voice as clearly as the clacking keys of her typewriter. I never asked her: What was it that I had dared? What was so terrible that I had dared to become?

BEING PRESENT

How many times have you been driving along in your car, or biking, or taking a long walk covering miles, a changing landscape, when you suddenly become aware that you have no recollection of the distance you've traveled, the sights you've passed without taking them in? Where were you? Oh, you were floating around, ruminating on something that happened yesterday, or five years ago, or about plans for tomorrow, or next summer, or even what to cook for dinner. We're so rarely in the present. A favorite yoga teacher often has us begin class in child's pose. As we lie there with our foreheads pressed to the mat, she'll tell us to *drop down. Drop in.*

Sometimes when I'm at my desk, I'll realize that I have contorted myself completely, and I haven't moved for hours, and that my legs have fallen asleep. I am elsewhere, not in my body, not in the room, not in my house. This may mean that I'm deeply engaged in the story I'm writing—that I have transported myself to the universe of my characters, but ideally, I want to be in both worlds: the one I've created in my mind, and also the one that's all around me. Because if I'm present, I will miss nothing. As writers, it is our job not only to imagine, but to witness. How are we meant to witness if we're not in the room?

Feel your feet on the ground. Your butt in the chair. Your elbows on the desk. Feel the pen in your hand, or the pads of your fingers against the computer's keys. Feel the breath moving in and out of your belly. The weight of your head on your neck. Your jaw: Is it clenched? Mine almost always is, unless I remind myself to release it. The further I get into this writing life, the more help I find I need. There are days when I am trapped in what Virginia Woolf called cotton wool: dazed, unfocused states in which the hours collapse, one flattening into the next. Days in which I am not entirely alive. Our minds have a tendency to wander. To duck and feint and keep us at a slight remove from the moment at hand. If we're writers or artists, we can't afford to live this way. We have to recognize the cotton wool, and cut through it.

My desk is covered with talismans: pieces of rose quartz, wishing stones from a favorite beach. Essential oils with names like *concentration* and *focus* and *inspiration*—the kind of thing I might have laughed at when I was younger. I could pretty much open up a new-age gift shop, if the writing thing ever dries up. But really, all that stuff is there to remind me to stay in the present, no matter how uncomfortable it is. Sometimes

I can hardly stand it—that *dropping in*. It's scary, boundless, infinite. It can feel like a free fall. But I know it's where my best work lies.

Each of us finds our own ritual to cut through the cotton wool. We can be gentle or harsh with ourselves. We can go for a run, or drop to the floor for twenty push-ups, or slam our fists down on our desks, or blare music until it's noisier than the noise inside of us. Hell, we can drink or do drugs—a short-term strategy that almost always ends badly. But whatever the ritual, we are attempting to see and hear and taste and smell and touch life around us. Otherwise, we escape ourselves, leaving our bodies behind like the shells of cicadas. Is it going to snow tomorrow? Was yesterday's meeting productive? Why did she say that to me? What did he mean by that? Who cares? We can't know. But it is in the present—not in the past, and most certainly not in the future—that we are able to see the landscape, to feel the range of our humanity, to travel every uncomfortable mile.

AMBITION

For a number of years, when I was on the faculty of a graduate writing program, each spring a large envelope filled with manuscripts—the work of prospective students—appeared in my mailbox. It was a competitive program, and only a few writers would be offered admission. I pored over each application carefully, as if I held in my hands nothing less than the fragile, beating heart of each person who had applied.

Of the hundreds of applications I evaluated, one stands out in memory: I began, as I always did, with a quick scan of the letters of recommendation, and then settled down to read the statement of purpose. Why did this writer want to pursue a graduate degree? The motivation for applying was an important factor in choosing successful candidates. I looked for passion, humility, kindness—qualities that would be valuable around a workshop table. I also kept an eye out for egoism, hubris, aggression.

I don't really see the point in studying writing, this statement began. *I've already been told by many people that I'm a genius.*

I shook my head, as if the words might rearrange themselves on the page. I read on:

I intend to become an internationally famous writer, to win a Guggenheim and live and work in the south of France.

I kept reading, fingers crossed that maybe this was a misguided attempt at a *New Yorker* "Shouts & Murmurs" column. But no. This guy wasn't kidding. The statement continued in the same vein. I don't remember the work—or even if I read it.

I was so annoyed as I looked around my overheated, cluttered academic office.

There's nothing wrong with ambition. We all want to win Guggenheims and live and write in the south of France, or some version thereof—don't we? But this can't be the goal. If we are thinking of our work as a ticket to a life of literary glamour, we really ought to consider doing something else. When I was first teaching, a student came up to me and asked if she should become a writer, or go work for Merrill Lynch. "Merrill Lynch!" I replied. Not because this student wasn't talented, but because she was even able to formulate that particular calculus.

The only reason to be a writer is *because you have to*. Most of the time, even if you've achieved publication and are lucky enough to be one of the few writers left in the country who are sent on book tour, you will find yourself in some small city where you know no one, in a hotel right off the highway that smells like room sanitizer, getting ready to give a reading where you might have an audience of five people sitting on folding chairs, two of whom work for the bookstore, two of whom are distant cousins of yours, and one of whom is a homeless person who gets up halfway through your reading and shuffles out. (True story.)

The real work involves a different kind of ambition: the creative kind. No writer I know is confident in her work. Just as Raymond Carver marked up his published stories with his red pencil, writers cringe when forced to reread our own prose; we're plagued by the certainty that we haven't quite achieved what we'd hoped we could. The work is only as good as our small, imperfect, pedestrian selves can make it. It exists in some idealized form, just out of reach. And so we push on. Driven by a desire to get it right, and the suspicion that there is no getting it right, we do our work in the hopes of coming close. There's no room in this process for an overblown ego. A career—whether it takes us to Cap d'Antibes or to the Staybridge Suites off the interstate—can be the result, but if it's the goal, we're lost before we've even begun.

Fog

E. L. Doctorow once compared writing to driving down a country road on a dark and foggy night. You can only see as far as your headlights, but you can make it all the way home just by slowly creeping along. So many of us, particularly fiction writers, think that it's our own dirty little secret: we're writing a novel or a story and *we can't see where it's going.* We think that other writers are the captains of their ships, navigating with a sense of clarity and purpose from one port to the next. But we—we have this shameful, idiosyncratic way of working in which we hardly know the next sentence.

Psst . . . guess what?

Unless we are writing a whodunit, or an intricately plotted thriller—writers rarely know where we're headed when we start out. I began my novel *Family History* with a character, a woman in her late thirties named Rachel Jensen, who was lying in bed in the middle of the afternoon, watching home movies. Clearly, something terrible had happened. But what? I thought it might involve her children and her marriage. She replayed home movies again and again, searching for clues. I searched for clues along with her, as she lay there in the darkness. Over the course of the two years it took me to write that novel, the story took shape one word at a time. I discovered what had happened to the Jensens just as if I were driving through that foggy night, keeping an eye out for signposts.

I always think I should know more. That I need more information. That I should outline, perhaps. Or do some research. But really, I need to remind myself that this not-knowing is at the heart of the creative endeavor. Paradoxically, the not-knowing is often what creates the energy, portent, and momentum in the piece of work itself. One of the truest pleasures for the writer alone in a room is when our characters surprise us by doing something unexpected. And so, as we are beginning, the most liberating thing we can do for ourselves is to exist in this state of heightened interest. It's a bit like standing at the edge of a playground, watching our children make their way in the world. What will they do next? What has happened to them? Do you really want to go over there? Who's the bully in the sandbox?

It requires faith in the process. The imagination has its own coherence. Our first draft will lead us. There's always time for thinking and shaping and restructuring later, after we've allowed something previously hidden to emerge on the page.

LUCK

I applied to college during my junior year of high school. I was sixteen—a very young and confused sixteen. My family's religious observance had hampered certain aspects of the usual teenage rebellion. While my friends were out in the woods drinking beer and smoking pot, I was sneaking off to eat a slice of bacon, sure that God would strike me dead. (To this day, I have an uneasy relationship with shellfish, afraid that I'll eat a bad shrimp and end up dying of anaphylactic shock.) I look back now and try to understand where I found the nerve to apply to college early. My parents didn't help me. They knew I was applying but they never thought I'd get in. I was a middling student, good at some subjects (English) and terrible at others (math). I was something of a pianist, having studied classical piano for most of my life, and I'm convinced it was this—the cassette tape of me playing Mozart's Sonata in A Major—that got me into better schools than my academic record deserved.

Why did I do it? I was desperate to get away from home. Life with my parents was unhappy. Though I wasn't aware of it at the time, I think I was afraid that if I didn't leave soon, I never would. Guilt and remorse would glue me to the spot. My parents' troubles seemed to be my fault. They fought over me as if they were two dogs and I was the bone. They each wanted me for their own, and in the process I was being trapped. To escape, I started to tell a lot of lies. I lied to my parents, to my friends, to my high school boyfriend, to Eddie Adler, to anyone who would listen. My own lies baffled me. I couldn't keep track of the stories I had told. Why was I making them up? Why was I pretending things had happened—often painful, dramatic things—when they hadn't?

The week before college acceptance letters were to be mailed out, I stopped eating. I was thin to begin with, and this hunger strike appeared to my well-meaning family pediatrician to be anorexia and so I was admitted to the hospital. I'm shaking my head as I write these words, because I know how it sounds—it must have been very serious for them to have hospitalized a sixteen-year-old girl who wasn't eating—but in truth, it was a tremendous overreaction, one of several that my parents had over the years, in which I was thought to be desperately ill. One time, a swollen gland in my neck led to a spinal tap and ultimately to surgery to remove the offending gland. And so I lay there at our small, local New Jersey hospital, being fed intravenously, until the morning my mother arrived at the hospital holding a thick, unopened envelope from Sarah Lawrence College.

I sat up and ate some soup and a few saltines. The intravenous lines were removed. I remember the dress I wore as I left the hospital on that warm April day: delicate, white, floaty. I was thin, but I felt strong, renewed. That envelope was my ticket out, and though a few more acceptances came in that week, my instinct told me that Sarah Lawrence—a small liberal arts college near New York City—was where I belonged. It's easy to make sense of it all in retrospect. To say: I knew I wanted to be a writer, that Sarah Lawrence had a faculty full of great writers who commuted there from New York City to teach, men and women who would become my mentors and surrogate parents, forever changing my life. To say: I had a plan for who I would become. But none of this was the case. Connecting the dots of a life can only be done backward, forensically. It's possible now to see how Eddie Adler, the lying, the starving, the white cotton dress, the thick envelope led—over the course of three decades—to the quiet house in the country, the piles of books, the husband and son, the solitary days. It's also possible to see that there are other ways it could have gone. Remove any of those elements—change a single detail—and the story spins off in another direction.

GUIDES

One of those working writers who was teaching at Sarah Lawrence when I first arrived was a short, sturdy woman with a cloud of white hair and the kindest face I'd ever seen. Grace Paley was legendary. She spoke the way she wrote, with the street cadence of a Brooklyn-raised Jewish immigrant's daughter, and she was wise, humble, gentle, and incisive. I often found myself on the verge of tears when I was in her presence.

I was a girl in need of a new family. I became one of Grace's many surrogate children. And though I wasn't ready—though it would be another six years and a whole lot of heartache before I began to change into the woman I'd hoped to become—I recognized in her then something I wanted: a feeling mind, a thinking heart. A lived life. I flailed around, aimless, self-destructive, deluded, and without hope for years after my first encounter with Grace, but I knew there was another way to be. I had seen it in her. I just didn't know how to get there.

I only had a few workshops with Grace in college and in graduate school, and they were often canceled, a note tacked to the door announcing that she was in jail again, imprisoned for civil disobedience, but her advice stayed with me. "If I love a sentence I've just written enough to get up and go into the other room to read it aloud to my husband, I know I should cut it," she once said. I didn't know what she meant at the time. Wasn't it good to love your sentences? Now I know she meant simply this: don't admire your own work, not while you're writing it. "I do my best writing in the bathtub," she said. I thought she meant she sat neck-deep in suds, scribbling. Now I realize that she was talking about the importance of getting away from the page to let the mind wander and solve problems. To this day, I'll think of some casual remark she made when I was her student, and I'll realize: *Oh, so that's what Grace meant.* She, among others, is in the room when I write. All my mentors—Esther Broner, Jerome Badanes—they're gone now, and writing their names here feels like a form of Yizkor, the Jewish prayer for the dead. They were—they became—my family.

If we keep our eyes open, we will encounter our true teachers. We don't even need to know them. Virginia Woolf is my teacher. I keep her near me in the form of her *A Writer's Diary.*

I flip the book open to a random page and encounter a kindred spirit who walked this road before me, and who—though her circumstances were vastly different from my own—makes me feel less isolated in the world. Though we are alone in our rooms, alone with our demons, our inner censors, our teachers remind us that we're not alone in the endeavor. We are part of a great tapestry of those who have preceded us. And so we must ask ourselves: Are we feeling with our minds? Thinking with our hearts? Making every empathic leap we can? Are we witnesses to the world around us? Are we climbing on the shoulders of those who paved the way for us? Are we using every last bit of ourselves, living these lives of ours, spending it, spending it all, every single day?

What You Know?

Sit around a scarred wooden table in a writing workshop for enough hours and you'll hear *write what you know,* along with *show don't tell, never use adverbs,* and other guidelines. And know that every rule you'll hear in a writing workshop is meant to be broken. You can do absolutely anything—tell, not show, make excellent use of an adverb—as long as you can pull it off. Get out there on the high wire, unafraid to fall. Who says you can't use ellipses or an exclamation point? Who says dialogue has to be indented and in quotation marks? Who says you can't write a whole novel from the point of view of a child trapped in a room?

What does this even mean: to write what you know? I can tell you that it makes some writers, when they're starting out, think that they can only write about what has happened to them. Then they panic. They worry that maybe their lives aren't dramatic enough. But can you imagine what our lives (or our work) would be like if we were only able to write directly out of our own experience? We'd have to live such interesting lives that we'd all flame out by age forty, collapsing from the exhaustion of chasing after new material.

There is a tremendous difference between writing from a place that haunts you, from the locus of your obsession and fear and desire—and writing about what you yourself have been through. We know more than we think we do. I am not, for instance, a sixty-four-year-old male psychoanalyst Holocaust survivor. But in my third novel, *Picturing the Wreck,* that is who I became. I was Solomon Grossman. "Emma Bovary, c'est moi," said Flaubert. I didn't question whether or not I could get inside the heart and soul of a man more than thirty years my senior, who had suffered in ways I hadn't suffered, taken pleasure in ways I hadn't. In the first pages, Solomon wakes up in the morning and masturbates. How did I give myself creative license to write such a scene? Because I *knew*. I knew what he would do, and how it would make him feel, before, during, and after. We are limited only by our capacity to empathize. We have all experienced sorrow, grief, loss, joy, euphoria, thirst, lust, injustice, envy, a broken heart.

Recently I tried on a space suit known as AGNES, an acronym for Age Gain Now Empathy System, designed by researchers at MIT to generate the feeling, for its wearer, of being elderly. I climbed into what looked like ski pants, which were attached by bungee cords to suspenders, limiting my range of motion. I wore a helmet that also connected to the suspenders by elastic cords, shrinking me and inhibiting my ability to turn my neck. There were goggles to obscure my vision. I stuffed my feet into slippers that had sharp plastic spikes on their soles, so that each step I took was painful.

It was a chance to walk a mile in someone else's shoes. An eighty- or perhaps ninety-year-old version of myself. A peek into what the future might hold. So this is what it would be like to pick up a spoon. To get up out of a chair. To climb a flight of stairs. And though I'm not sure I needed to experience AGNES in order to imagine the physical experience of being old and frail, it sharpened my perspective. I thought differently about that hunched-over man trying to cross Broadway as the "Don't Walk" sign flashes, or the woman with dementia who escapes her assisted living facility and finds herself disoriented on the side of a highway. I haven't yet lived these moments, and perhaps I never will. But I know what it is to be alone. To be lost. To be afraid.

PIANO

Every Wednesday after school, my mother drove me a half-hour to a neighboring town for my piano lesson. On our way, we stopped at a Howard Johnson's and I ordered a swiss chocolate almond ice-cream cone. I don't remember much about our car rides—I can't summon up a single conversation—but I do remember the precise taste of the ice cream, the satisfying crunch of the almonds. The sensory details of our childhoods are often what remain vivid: the glare of the late afternoon sun, the steady *whoosh* of the highway below, the car's upholstery against my back, the sight of my mother's hands—no longer young—on the steering wheel. She drove an enormous, dark brown Cadillac Eldorado. Why? I don't know. My parents weren't showy people. If I were creating a character like my mother, I wouldn't have her drive an Eldorado.

My piano lesson was the punctuation—a comma, perhaps, or better yet a semicolon—in the middle of my week. The rest of life paused on either side of it. Mr. Tipton was passionate, exacting, wounded if a student came to a lesson unprepared. He had bright red hair and a ruddy face, as did Mrs. Tipton, and they had a brood of red-headed Tiptons. I cared a lot about what Mr. Tipton thought, and I tried never to be unprepared. When I practiced piano, my usual fears and anxieties fell away. Did Sol Kimpinski really have a crush on me? Did I have a crush on him? Had I studied enough for my American history exam? Was my father—so pale, so overweight, so unhappy—about to have a heart attack and die?

At my upright Mason & Hamlin piano in the den where my father spent the evenings hanging in traction, I practiced for hours every day. I ran through my scales and arpeggios, then turned to whatever piece of music I was working on: a Bach Invention, a Chopin nocturne, a Beethoven bagatelle, a Mozart sonata. I didn't consider the meaning of the word *practice*. It would be many years before I began to understand that all of life is practice: writing, driving, hiking, brushing teeth, packing lunch boxes, making beds, cooking dinner, making love, walking dogs, even sleeping. We are always practicing. Only practicing.

For a while, I thought I might want to be a pianist when I grew up. I thought this the way my son Jacob wants to be a professional basketball player. Or the way my mother wanted to be a famous writer. It was a romantic daydream; I had a little bit of talent, a pretty good ear, some dedication. I see now that piano was my training ground—at least as important as any writing workshop. I was preparing myself for a lifetime of working with words. The phrasing, the pauses, the crescendos and diminuendos, keeping time, the creating of shape, the coaxing out of a tonal quality. All these are with me as I approach the page.

When you have written something—whether part of a story, a poem, an essay, an opening for a longer piece, anything that feels like it might be a keeper—listen to it. What does it sound like? Read your words aloud. Even if you look like a crazy person, it doesn't matter. No one's watching. Pay attention to the way the language moves. Is it creating the effect you're after? I think of some of Nabokov's sentences, or the end of Delmore Schwartz's "In Dreams Begin Responsibilities." Fluid sentence-rivers, carrying us along on a current of commas, faster, faster until we are nearly breathless. Or the atonal juxtapositions of Don DeLillo's. Or the clean, staccato beats of Hemingway, a period like a knife jab in the gut. What instrument does your language call to mind? A cello? An electric guitar? An oboe? Are you writing a concerto? A symphony? A lullaby? Listen and you will begin to hear the rhythms of your own voice.

FIVE SENSES

A character is taking a walk—say, down a winding path in the countryside. That character is lost in thought. We get memory, wistfulness, longing, regret. This character—let's call him Joe—is on his way to his girlfriend's house. They've had a fight and he's hoping to make up with her. He's thinking about how he'll apologize to her, what she'll say, whether the day will turn out well. But in the meantime, Joe is walking. His good city shoes are caked with mud from the previous night's rain. A bumblebee buzzes in the nearby honeysuckle. The scent wafts over him, reminding him of a happier time with the girlfriend, a picnic they took last summer. He has a slight sniffle. His nose is running. He stuffs his hands deep into his pockets, looking for a tissue, but instead finds a wrapper from a fortune cookie. His stomach rumbles. He wonders if she'll offer him anything to eat.

For us to feel Joe's essential humanness, we must have access to his body. This is one of the simplest ways to bring a character to life on the page, and yet we so easily forget. If we inhabit his body as he walks down the path, things will happen in the writing: the bumblebee, the honeysuckle, the fortune cookie.

His musings will be associative, connected to the corporeal present. After all, what else is there? We see, smell, taste, hear, and touch. The senses are gateways to our inner lives.

A friend once told me about a walk she took through Washington Square Park in New York City on an early spring day. It was a route she took regularly, from her home to her office, but on this day she stopped dead in the middle of the park, overcome by a panic attack. What had happened? Why that moment? Her heart raced and she tried to catch her breath. It seemed the world was dissolving around her. When she was finally able to sit down on a park bench, she realized that the quality of the air and the sunlight were precisely the same as they had been a year before—a year to the day—when she had been diagnosed with breast cancer. She had made a full recovery and until that moment she hadn't remembered that it was the anniversary of her diagnosis. But her body remembered. The light, the air. The breeze against her skin. A street band playing in the distance. Her body brought her back to that place of terror, to a time that her mind resisted.

Write the words "The Five Senses" on an index card and tack it to a bulletin board above your desk. You should have a bulletin board above your desk, if at all possible. Some place where you can tack images, quotes, postcards, scraps of thoughts and ideas that will help remind you of who you are and what you're doing. When it comes to building a character, to grounding one in a place and time, ask: What does she smell right now? What does the air feel like against her bare arms? Is there a siren in the distance? A slamming door? A car alarm? Is she thirsty? Hung over? Does her back ache? Not all of this needs to end up on the page. But you need to know. Because knowing your character's five senses will open up the world around her. It may even unlock the story itself.

BAD DAYS

Some of my worst writing days have been the ones that stretched out before me in all their glory. No doctor's appointments, no plumber coming to fix the bathroom leak, no early pickup for my son at school. Not even a pesky fly banging against the lamp shade. Eight clear hours. Just me and the silence. Me and the dogs asleep at my feet. Me and the scented candle, the fire roaring in the fireplace. Me and . . .

Well, you see the problem: that little word, *me*. Wherever we go, to borrow a phrase from the Buddhist writer Jon Kabat-Zinn, there we are. It is easy to get in our own way. We can promise ourselves that we're just going to check this one e-mail (make this bed, cook this sauce, run this errand) and before we know it, we have been swept away from our work as if by a rogue wave. We grow angrier as the day progresses this way. How can we be letting this happen? How, when circumstances were so damned perfect?

Sometimes, it's those perfect circumstances that can be the most oppressive. In another life—before motherhood—I spent months at a time at artists' colonies—those bucolic, faraway places where lunch is dropped off at your cabin in the woods, and silence is the rule during daytime hours. Composers, painters, sculptors, poets, novelists all living and breathing their work—but I remember the difficulty I always had, settling into an ideal work environment. Especially if I'd headed off into the woods to attempt something new. In the endless quiet, my inner censor's voice grew louder. A composer friend was once shown to his studio at a famous colony by a man who told him that Aaron Copland had composed *Appalachian Spring* in that same room. My friend spent the ensuing weeks staring out the window, mired in self-doubt. Sometimes we're better off with just enough time. Or even not enough time.

When my son was little, he loved a book by Judith Viorst called *Alexander and the Terrible, Horrible, No Good, Very Bad Day*. Poor Alexander. He woke up with gum in his hair, he ended up in the middle seat during carpool, his mom forgot to pack dessert in his lunch box, he had a cavity at the dentist, and just when he thought things couldn't get any worse, he saw people kissing on television. You can feel the momentum of a day like that turning against you, and if it does, sometimes the best thing to do is crawl back into bed and wait for it to pass.

We have to learn to be kind to ourselves. What we're doing isn't easy. We have chosen to spend the better part of our lives in solitude, wrestling with our deepest thoughts and obsessions and concerns. We unleash the beast of memory; we peer into Pandora's box. We do all this in the spirit of faith and exploration, with no guarantee that what we produce will be worthwhile. We don't call in sick. We don't take mental health days. We don't get two weeks paid vacation, or summer Fridays, or holiday weekends. Often, we are out of step with the tempo of those around us. It can feel isolating and weird. And so, when the day turns against us, we might do well to follow the advice of the Buddhist writer Sylvia Boorstein, who talks to herself as if she's a child she loves very much. *Sweetheart,* she'll say. *Darling. Honey. That's all right. There, there. Go take a walk. Take a bath. Take a drive. Bake a cake. Nap a little. You'll try again tomorrow.*

MESS

I had just turned seventeen when I went off to college, and though I may have looked the part of a freshman, I was immature and confused. The rules of my strict upbringing had defined me and kept me in place. In casting those rules aside—no longer worried that God might be watching—I was on my own, and as prepared for it as a toddler crossing a city street by herself. They say that the cerebral frontal cortex—the part of the brain that identifies and comprehends risk and danger—is not fully developed until well into one's twenties. Risk and danger—these were mere abstractions. I never even considered that actions produce consequences.

I entered a self-destructive spiral that lasted six years and involved drugs, alcohol, and a powerful married man, the step-father of one of my closest friends. He was also a sociopath who eventually served time in prison for tax evasion and embezzlement. Read that again. Slowly. Try to make sense of it. Mistress of a married man. A married *criminal* man. I didn't rebel by half-measures. Once I began, there was no stopping me. Anything could have happened, and a lot did, none of it pretty. Certainly, observing me during that time, few would have laid odds on my growing up to become a novelist and memoirist, a professor, a contented wife and mother living in rural Connecticut. Life doesn't follow narrative arcs that stretch from one predictable scene to the next—does it? The landmark documentary Up series, by Michael Apted, in which he follows a group of British schoolchildren beginning at age seven, and then every seven years up through middle age, has the tag line: *Give me the child until age seven, and I will give you the man.*

Well, yes and no. If we examine a moment's interactions and details, we can cast out lines, like fishermen; there are infinite ways a life might unfold. If someone were to have observed me at age seven, the trajectory through my early twenties might have shown up like the faintest crease a fortune-teller might see in the palm of a hand. If someone had drawn an arrow from my parents' unhappiness back through my family's history, which included some alcoholism, drug abuse, depression, and a complex legacy of secrets, then perhaps one could have imagined a rough patch down the road. But, as in the blooming of an orchid or the metastasis of a tumor, the conditions had to be right. If I hadn't crossed paths with that particular man would something else, equally or perhaps even uglier, have happened? Or would the shadow of that particular danger have passed over me? Throw any variable into the mix—a phone call, a different turn, a stranger walking into the room, a new friend, a caring mentor, a thunderstorm, a broken lock—and everything changes. Suddenly you're telling a different story.

What happened next could not have been etched into the palm of any hand. The winter of the year I was twenty-three, my parents were driving home during a blizzard and my father passed out behind the wheel of their car. My mother was in the passenger seat. He was wearing a seat belt. She was not. Two weeks later, my father died from his injuries. By the time my mother was pried by the jaws of life from the wrecked car, she had eighty broken bones. In my memoir *Slow Motion,* I write about my parents' accident. I write about being a twenty-three-year-old college drop out trying to disengage myself from my married boyfriend, subsisting on a diet of white wine and scotch and saltines. I write about my grief at the loss of my father; taking care of my mother; ending, finally, my destructive relationship; returning to college. On the cover of a paperback edition of *Slow Motion,* the subtitle reads: "a memoir of a life rescued by tragedy." This is marketing-speak, fraught and complex events reduced to a sound bite. The tragedy of my parents' accident changed everything for me, but it didn't rescue me.

What is true is that I became a writer. It had begun many years earlier, under the covers, with a flashlight, scribbling letters filled with lies. It had roots in my solitary childhood. It grew within the girl of seven, fourteen, twenty-one. But after the accident, conditions were right. I was broken open, no longer innocent or oblivious. I had a story to tell—a story I was not necessarily ready to tell, but that didn't matter. (Fail, fail better.) I was compelled to follow every faint crease, to become a student and translator of my experience. To reach into the past. To continue my relationship with my father on the page, to keep him—to keep all of them who died during that long, impossible year, including my grandmother and two uncles—alive. Language became my navigational tool. With every word, I pulled myself a little bit further out of the abyss. With every sentence, my focus sharpened. With every story, I began to form myself from the inside out.

Writing in the Dark

I wrote my first novel in a borrowed room down the hall from my tiny New York City apartment. Each morning, I would pad barefoot to that room, still in my pajamas, a mug of steaming coffee in my hand. I spent a couple of years there, smoking cigarettes, staring out the window into the interior courtyard. I'd write, smoke. Write, smoke some more. I felt pressure, yes, but the pressure had entirely to do with the novel itself, and not with the outside world. The outside world did not yet exist for me. I wasn't thinking about editors and agents and literary success. There was no Facebook or Twitter. I didn't know the first thing about the business of writing. Of course I cared about being published. I had a lot to prove—to myself and to others. I wanted the affirmation that I wasn't deluded. I needed to show my shattered mother, my fractured family, my dead father, and my skeptical friends that I might amount to something after all. But it was the work itself that drew me in, then threw me a lifeline and saved me.

Remember, as you begin, that you are in a remote and exotic place—the literary equivalent of far eastern Bhutan. It's a place where no one can find you. Where anything is possible. Where, for a time, you are free, liberated from the expectations and ideas of others. You are trekking, and the vistas are infinite. This freedom is necessary whether you're working on your first book or your tenth. In order to create a world on the page, you need to push away from the world around you. You must forget its expectations and constraints.

The time when you're working on a first book is when the darkness is at its purest and most precious. Someday you may look back on it with longing. No one has yet pinned you to a tradition, told you who you are. You can't troll the Internet for reviews or commentary about yourself. In the dark, you are free to grow like a moon flower, to experiment without consequences. There are no limits, no definitions. What are your obsessions? In what recesses of your psyche will you find your voice? What rules can you break? Where is the edge and how can you form your work against it? It's all ahead of you, and this time in the dark will allow you to find out.

I have spent my writing life trying to get back to the feeling I had in that room in New York City more than twenty years ago. I find it, then lose it, then find it again. I'm a cave dweller, thriving in the most secluded of regions, but I also have a family, students, friends, responsibilities. And so I have tricks and tools. We all do. We shut off the Internet, turn off our phones. We compare brands of earplugs. We pack ourselves off to cabins hidden in the woods. I remember a time when, suddenly, reviews of my work began with a paragraph about the kinds of books I write. I seemed to have reached some sort of midcareer retrospective without having any idea how I'd gotten there. I discovered that I didn't want to know how I was being perceived. When I'm alone in my writing room, I don't want to be thinking about what kind of writer I am. What do "they" think are my strengths, my weaknesses? What are my "themes"? In a dark, quiet space, the world recedes.

There is only one opportunity to write in complete darkness: when you're at the beginning. Use it. Use it well. The loneliest day in the life of a published writer may be publication day. Nothing happens. Perhaps your editor sends flowers.

Maybe not. Maybe your family takes you out for dinner. But the world won't stop to take notice. The universe is indifferent. You have put the shape of your soul between the covers of a book and no one declares a national holiday. Someone named Booklover gives you a one-star review on Amazon.com.

So what is it about writing that makes it—for some of us—as necessary as breathing? It is in the thousands of days of trying, failing, sitting, thinking, resisting, dreaming, raveling, unraveling that we are at our most engaged, alert, and alive. Time slips away. The body becomes irrelevant. We are as close to consciousness itself as we will ever be. This begins in the darkness. Beneath the frozen ground, buried deep below anything we can see, something may be taking root. Stay there, if you can. Don't resist. Don't force it, but don't run away. Endure. Be patient. The rewards cannot be measured. Not now. But whatever happens, any writer will tell you: This is the best part.

"You climb a long ladder until you can see over the roof, or over the clouds. You are writing a book. You watch your shod feet step on each round rung, one at a time; you do not hurry and do not rest."

—ANNIE DILLARD

Building the Boat

I was in the middle of my second novel and struggling. Instead of engagement, I felt a nagging worry. Had I lost my way? Maybe I had taken a wrong turn—but where? One afternoon, I met a friend of mine, a poet and novelist, for coffee.

"I feel like I'm in a boat in the middle of the ocean and there's no land in sight," I told him.

He took a sip of his drink and peered at me over his glasses.

"Yeah," he said. "And you're building the boat."

Courage

John Updike once called fiction "nothing less than the subtlest instrument for self-examination and self-display that mankind has invented." Engagement with this most subtle of instruments requires a daily summoning of stamina, optimism, discipline, and hope. We are in the ocean, yes. We are constructing the very thing that holds us. We have nothing to latch on to. If beginnings and ends are shorelines, middles are where we dive deep, where we patch holes, where we risk drowning. This is no time for half measures. We must meet the page with everything we've got. We must lay every last bit of ourselves on the line, to, in the words of Annie Dillard, "spend it all, shoot it, play it, lose it, all, right away, every time."

You might think this requires fearlessness. I used to think so, too, which was a problem because I am anything but fearless. Shellfish, bees, thunderstorms, airplanes, snakes, bears, random allergic reactions, black ice are only a few of my phobias. I am not a risk taker, not in the physical sense. You won't catch me hang gliding, or even waterskiing. But when I'm alone in a room—say, on the chaise longue, from which I haven't budged since my first cup of coffee, the sky an overcast gray, the house empty—I am compelled to take risks. Because there's no point, really, in spending one's life alone in a room, out of rhythm with the rest of humanity, unless the stakes are high. What will today bring? I hold my breath, dive down. Come to the surface, gasping, empty-handed. I catch my breath, then dive again. Maybe this time. I reach for treasures in this underwater landscape. Ones that only I can see. Ones that, should I discover them, will be mine and mine alone. I suppose this requires a certain kind of courage. But courage and fearlessness are not the same thing. Courage is all about feeling the fear and *doing it anyway*.

Who would sign up for such a life? Most days it feels like lunacy. Sometimes it occurs to me that not everyone in the world spends their time in this manner. That it probably isn't healthy. I have a lot of friends who are writers, and I think we recognize in each other a slight shell-shocked, glazed-over quality, a sensitivity—possibly covered up by humor or defensiveness or a few drinks—that comes from our daily grappling with the page, that subtle instrument of self-examination. My husband used to be a foreign correspondent, and when he gets together with other foreign correspondents, inevitably conversation turns to a particular bar in Nairobi, or a street battle in Mogadishu, or the merits of a particular bodyguard. They speak a language only they understand. The same is true with my writer friends. *How's it going?* The question is proffered delicately. *What are you working on?* We watch one another keenly, like soldiers keeping an eye out for one another on the battlefield. Are we holding it together? Are we growing? Are we forging new ground? Or have we succumbed to fear? Are we using irony as a defense? Or falling into self-parody? Have we become too clever, too cynical, too sentimental?

Unlike other artists—dancers, sculptors, or cellists, say—as long as we hold onto our faculties, writers can continue to grow creatively until we die. The middle of a writing life is much like being in the midst of a book itself. Here we often discover our weaknesses and our strengths. Here we are in the hard, hard work of articulating the story itself. And, just as our lives are shaped by moments, hours, and the passing of days, stories are shaped by sentences. By movements of characters through time. By the quiet tenacity with which we enter the stepping stone of each word.

This kind of tenacity is not a static state, an exotic destination to which you travel and then cross off the list. Each and every day that you approach the page, you are reaching for it once again. At times, it will elude you. At times, it will seem to have abandoned you. But in the face of this, be persistent, dogged, patient, determined. Remember that this moment, this day, is one stitch in a tapestry of days. Remember that you cannot—*should* not—see the shape unfolding before you. Spend it all anyway. Gamble with your whole self.

MUSES

Though it defied the natural order of things, I always believed my mother would outlive me. After my father's death, even the smallest exchange between us exploded into a battle of wills. It seemed there was only room in this world for one of us—and when it came to survival, she was the stronger, tougher one. On the dedication page of my first memoir, *Slow Motion*—though my mother was barely speaking to me at the time of its publication—I wrote that she had taught me something about survival. Faint praise? That I am here—on the chaise longue, in the house on the hill, my son at school, my husband at his writing office in the village down the road, the dogs, yes, the dogs, asleep at my feet, their bones making a deeply comforting *thunk* as they sink to the floor—the very fact that I am here—my computer balanced on my lap, the half-finished cappuccino, the midlife reading glasses pinching my nose, the pile of galleys and student work to be read on the table next to me—that I am here writing, and my mother is dead, continues to amaze me.

It was just the two of us. She demanded loyalty, which effectively meant distancing myself from the rest of my family, with whom she didn't get along. After six months in rehab, she recovered from her injuries and I moved her into a rental apartment on West End Avenue in New York City, just a few blocks from where I lived. She remained on the Upper West Side—in various apartments on Riverside Drive, and later, on West Eighty-sixth Street—until she died eighteen years later. Still, today, when I am in that neighborhood, I see an elderly woman. She's being pushed by an aide in a wheelchair, or she's using a cane, or she's striding down Broadway. Something in her regal posture—the proud lift of her chin, her chic bouclé jacket—reminds me of my mother and for an instant I think that it's all been a mistake. She's not dead after all. She fooled us—the coroner, the funeral parlor, my husband who identified her body—and she's returned to haunt me. She's at Zabar's, picking up some French Roast. She's sitting outside Le Pain Quotidien on a warm spring day, in a dark coat and sunglasses. For years after she died, when the phone rang I still checked the caller ID, screening for her name.

Shapiro writes about matriarchy.
Shapiro writes about mothers and daughters.
About estrangement.
About the complexity of familial love.

My mother can be found in most of my work. I have written countless essays and stories in which she figures, directly or indirectly. She once tracked me down in a beauty salon in New York City where I was getting a bikini wax. I had been avoiding my mother—and she burst through the door to confront me. A short story eventually emerged from that moment. How could it not? She has been—more than any other person in my life—my muse. It has been said that the blessing is next to the wound. All my life, I have attempted to peel back the layers. I do so not out of anger, or recrimination, or revenge, but rather, in the hope—tears are in my eyes as I write this—that under all those layers I will find something tender and genuine, something I can hold in my hands like a fragile baby bird. *There, there,* I will whisper if I ever locate it. *We didn't do such a good job of this. Let's try again.*

TRUST

At some point, it becomes impossible to see our own work clearly. We've gone over our sentences so many times that their very meaning begins to break apart and become just squiggles and lines on the page. We've worked for so many months on a draft that we now have it committed to memory, and it seems carved in stone. Immutable. Irrevocable. We no longer see clunky language or typos. Why are so many characters wearing bathrobes? Or clearing their throats? Or eating pasta?

We all need outside readers. Each one of us benefits from a fresh set of eyes. But how do we know when we've reached this point? Some writers only show their work when they've finished multiple drafts of it. Others share on a regular basis with a trusted reader. My husband Michael is my first reader, and most evenings I read him a bit of what I'm working on. The most I'll ever get out of him in the way of praise is a long pause, followed by "good," or the rare "that was really fucking great." Most of the time, he has notes for me. These notes can range from comments about word choice, to issues with the structure, or concerns about cloudy logic. Sometimes I bristle—but usually I come around. The main thing is, I know he wants me to write the best book I possibly can. We're in this together. And he possesses none of the characteristics that are to be avoided when thinking of considering early readers for your work: envy. Indifference. Comparison. Laziness. Dishonesty. Lousy bedside manner. Secret agenda. Rudeness. Hostility. Poor boundaries. False enthusiasm. Lack of discernment. Inattentiveness. Distractibility. Did I mention envy?

We're so vulnerable when we share new work. I once had a student who was unfazed speaking in front of huge audiences for her job as a CEO. But the first time she read a piece of her memoir aloud in my small private workshop, her voice shook, her hands trembled, and her eyes welled up. So much is on the line. We've revealed ourselves on these fledgling pages. The unconsidered response can be devastating. I have had wonderful readers over the years, and destructive ones. Once I made the mistake of showing a piece of a novel to a colleague too early, and her comments—while meant to be helpful and supportive—were so off the mark that they derailed me. I've also made the mistake of giving pages of a new piece to a writer who was unaccustomed to being in that position, and who treated them in a cavalier manner (she glanced at them and called me from her cell phone while at a hair salon), which both hurt and offended me.

I remember the first time I left my infant in the arms of a friend to run across the street to buy diapers. She was about to be a mother herself, had nieces and nephews—she knew her way around babies—but still, entrusting my weeks-old infant to her for ten minutes felt nearly impossible. It can feel the same with a manuscript. It's your baby, after all. So choose your early readers wisely. Think about your reasons for sharing. Examine your own motives. Why now? Are you ready? Or are you just trying to impress someone? Do you want to be told that you're a genius? (I once slogged through eight hundred pages of a friend's first draft, then discovered that he had been anticipating only praise. When I told him that there were far too many female characters on their knees performing mind-blowing oral sex, our conversation was over, and the friendship unfathomably lost.)

Ask yourself: Why this person? Will she treat my manuscript with respect? Read it with close attention? If you find one or two genuinely helpful readers—ones who are able to speak with you about your work in a way that helps you—consider yourself lucky. Return the favor whenever you can. When we apply what we know to the manuscript pages of a friend, when we do our best to understand what the writer hopes to accomplish, we are completing the circle. We do this for each other because there is precious little we *can* do for each other. We're alone in our rooms, in our heads. But we can reach out a hand. Who better than us? After all, we've been there, too.

Rhythm

Three pages a day, five days a week. When working on a book, this has been my pattern for my entire writing life. I spend most mornings writing my three pages, and I revisit them in the afternoon. I scribble in the margins, thoughts about edits, word choices. Sometimes I reread them before I go to sleep. I cross out paragraphs, I rearrange sentences. I ask questions that I hope to answer in the light of the next day. These pages are where I begin the following morning, because those notes give me a way in. If I begin by implementing the changes, before I know it I'm back inside the manuscript, already at work. I've evaded the pitfalls and distractions that often lie in wait for me.

Some writers count words. Others fill a certain number of pages, longhand, have a set number of hours they spend at their desk. It doesn't matter what the deal is that you strike with yourself, as long as you keep up your end of it, that you establish a working routine for yourself, a rhythm. I prefer to think of it as rhythm rather than discipline. Discipline calls to my mind a taskmaster, perhaps wielding a whip. Discipline has a whiff of punishment to it, or at least the need to cross something off a list, the way my son Jacob does with his homework. (Big sigh. *Got it done.*) Rhythm, however, is a gentle aligning, a comforting pattern in our day that we know sets us up ideally for our work.

Three pages a day, five days a week. Do the math. I do, all the time. Fifteen pages a week. Sixty pages a month! A novel-length manuscript in half a year! Let me stop you right there. I have never written a novel-length manuscript in half a year. In fact, two years would be fast for me, and usually it's closer to three years, or more. So what has happened to my well-established rhythm?

I'll tell you what happens: it fails, it falls apart, it gets interrupted. William Styron once referred to this quandary as the "the fleas of life." He went on to say that "writers ever since writing began have had problems, and the main problem narrows down to just one word—*life*." The dog has a vet appointment; the school play is being performed at noon; it's flu season, a snow day; who knew there were so many long weekends? The roof springs a leak; the neighbor's house is under construction; a friend calls in a crisis. Life doesn't pause to make room for our precious writing time. Life stops for nothing, and we make accommodations. There is no stasis, no normal, no such thing as a regular day; only this attempt to create a methodology. Having a rhythm is no magic pill. Without a doubt, we will be pulled away. At times we will be frustrated and unproductive. But if we have our one way of working—a number of pages, or hours, or words—we will eventually return to it. This return won't be easy. The page is indifferent to us—no, worse. The page turns from us like a wounded lover. We will have to win it over, coax it out of hiding. Promise to do better next time. Apologize for our disregard. And then, we settle into the pattern that we know. Three pages. Two hours. A thousand words. We have wandered and now we are back. There is comfort in the familiar. We can do this. Breathe in, breathe out. Once again, just as we've been doing all along.

COMPOSING

Most of us compose directly on screens at some point in the writing process. Desktops, laptops, iPads, and variations thereof. Walk into any Starbucks, or down the aisle of any train or plane and there we are, our faces made ghostly by the bluish-white light cast from our devices. But the screen can make our work look neat and tidy—finished—before it is. We can swoop in, search and replace, cut and paste, highlight, delete, and all the while the screen absorbs the changes and still looks the same. If you've never tried it, see what happens if you write a draft of something longhand. Before long, you'll be forced to *x* out whole sentences. You'll draw circles and as-terisks and arrows. You'll change your mind about what you've crossed out, and write "stet" in the margin. It will look messy, because it *is* messy. It should be that: a beautiful, complicated mess. Who knows? Maybe only one sentence will remain. Maybe the whole order will be upended. You'll be able to see a road map of your progress as you build the architecture of your story. The poet Mark Strand has made art of his drafts on canvas, in which doodles and scribbles and columns fill up the space with what the poet Jorie Graham calls "a mildly feverish black cursive."

This fever is lost on the screen. The evidence of the mind making the thing—made visible in the cross outs, the thick rewriting of words over other words, the fanciful sketches—a cloud, a camel, a man in a hat—that seem to ride the waves of language, the places where the pen grows dark and forceful, nearly stabbing in its intensity. This is work being made in real time. Work that reveals its scars.

But—unless we are poets—there are practical consid-erations to writing longhand. Your hand gets a cramp. You become afraid of losing the notebook. Though I begin most of my creative work in a notebook, when I reach thirty or forty pages, I type a draft into my computer. What if there was a fire? A flood? The irony that my work stored on a *cloud* feels safer than the solid weight of a spiral-bound notebook, does not escape me. But at least for a while, the circles and squiggles, the *x*'d out sentences, the asterisks and inserts covering every inch of every page have served their purpose. They remind me that my work is changeable. That there is *play* in this thing I'm doing. I'm a child, finger-painting. This color? Why not? There is joy—rather than industry—in putting pen to paper. A sense of possibility, discovery.

For the past dozen years, I have used a particular brand of spiral-bound notebook—dark blue, the insignia of a prep school I did not attend emblazoned on its cover. I've become a little obsessive about these notebooks. They can only be found in one bookstore, in my in-laws' hometown. Whenever I visit, I stop by the prep school bookstore and stock up. I carry home armloads of them. I live in fear of running out, or—horrible thought—that they might be discontinued. Why these notebooks? They're nothing special to look at. I have no connection to the school, other than its location in the town where my husband grew up. The reason I'm attached to them is simple: the first time I randomly happened to write in one of those notebooks, the work went well.

We are, many of us, superstitious creatures. We think there may be reasons our day flows in the right direction. A favorite necklace, a penny found on the sidewalk, a crystal we tuck into our pocket, a private mantra—we may rely on talismans to help us along. But I've never heard a writer feel that way about a device with a screen. Oh sure, they're functional, practical. We would be lost without them. But just as we need to feel our feet on the earth, smell and taste the world around us, the pen scratching against the page, sensory and slow, is the difference between looking at a high-definition picture of a flower and holding that very same flower in your palm, feeling the brush of its petals, the color of its stamen rubbing off on your fingers.

Pick a notebook, any notebook. If you compose well in it, you will become attached. Choose a pen that feels right. It could be a beautiful, expensive fountain pen, or any old BIC. Whatever feels good in your hand. Okay—this is your notebook, and this is your pen. Balance the notebook on your lap or set it on a table. And wherever you are in your work, start there. If you listen closely, you'll hear the sound the pen makes as it moves across the page. Now, doodle something. Write a few sentences. Scratch them out. Write a few more.

CHANGE

I had just published *Slow Motion* when Jacob was born. In the first sentence of that memoir, I refer to my parents' car crash as the event that divided my life into before and after. What

I didn't know—I was in my early thirties and single when I began the book, in my midthirties and engaged to be married when I finished—is that a life containing only a single "before and after" moment is indeed a fortunate one. "My life closed twice before its close," said Emily Dickinson. After my father's death, I carried those words around in the back pages of my Filofax for years. I intuited the truth in them, though I couldn't have yet imagined how a life could close twice—or even more—before its close. I thought it was kind of like a one-per-customer thing.

But then, when Jacob was six months old, he developed seizures that led to a diagnosis of a rare and nearly always catastrophic disorder known as Infantile Spasms. Seven out of a million babies are diagnosed each year with this disorder, and only 15 percent of them survive. Most are left blind, physically impaired, or brain damaged. As I sat in the doctor's office hearing these dire statistics about the infant I was holding in my arms—*pain engraves a deeper memory*—everything I cared about in the world was distilled into a single moment. Looking down at my only child on that late autumn afternoon, I knew that if he wasn't okay—if he wasn't part of that small percentage of babies who make it—that my life would be over. I believed the loss of a child would be the only pain from which it would be impossible to recover. And in that doctor's office I was staring straight into the dark heart of that likely outcome.

Over the next weeks—a frenzy of trying to calibrate the experimental medication that came via FedEx from Canada, of doses around the clock, of waking a sleeping baby at three o'clock in the morning to drink down the medicine that was or wasn't going to save him, and then the months of vigilance that followed: was that a seizure or just a hiccup?—my usual way of moving through life was no longer possible. I could not hover at an outsidery distance. I was not filing away details for later. Being a writer offered me no protection. In Lorrie Moore's story "People Like That Are the Only People Here," a surgeon tells a writer-mother that her baby has a Wilms' Tumor. ("Is that apostrophe *s* or *s* apostrophe," she asks.) The writer argues with her husband, who wants her to sell a story about it. She calls what is happening to them "a nightmare of narrative slop."

I had always shaped narratives out of my life's most painful and difficult circumstances. I had held to a belief—as necessary to me as a heartbeat—that this was a redemptive act; to create a coherent narrative out of sorrow or grief was genuine and worthwhile. But as I fought for the survival of my own child the failures of narrative seemed to taunt me. John Banville wrote about *Blue Nights,* Joan Didion's memoir about the death of her only daughter: "Against life's worst onslaughts, nothing avails, not even art. Especially not art."

Each day, I climbed the stairs of our Brooklyn brownstone

to my third-floor office and stared blankly at the wall. I was a writer who couldn't write. A writer who didn't see the point of writing. Words on paper couldn't save my child, and they could no longer save me. It felt as if I had chosen to spend my life in the most frivolous way possible, making up stories. *Narrative slop.* Why wasn't I the research scientist who had invented the drug that was stalling our son's seizures? Now *that* was important. What if he had decided to become a poet instead? What then?

But writing was how my husband and I both made our livings, and we had a mortgage and doctors' bills. I *had* to write. I had no choice. I continued to stare at the wall until—it took the better part of a year—a story started to form at the center of the most shaken place inside of me. As my boy began to heal, I began to write a novel about maternal anxiety. What else was there? I was a big, quivering heap of maternal anxiety. I wondered if I would ever find any other subject interesting, ever again. Love and the terrifying, concomitant potential of loss, were, for a long time, my only subject. I had been forever altered by our brush with catastrophe. It was written on my body. My instrument had changed. And I now understood that it would continue to change. That there would be more befores and afters ahead. Fighting it was futile, impossible. Accepting, even embracing this, was the true work, not only of being a writer, but of being alive.

BEGINNING AGAIN

We may be halfway through a novel, an essay, a story, or a memoir or we may be nearing the finish line on a piece that has taken us years. But wherever we are in our work, we have never been exactly here, today. Today, we need to relearn what it is that we do. We have to remind ourselves to be patient, gentle with our foibles, ruthless with our time, withstanding of our frustrations. We remember what it is that we need. The solitude of an empty home, a walk through the woods, a bath, or half an hour with a good book—the echo of well-formed sentences in our ears. Whatever it takes to begin again.

When I was first learning to meditate, this idea of beginning again was revelatory. It still is. The meditation teacher Sharon Salzberg speaks of catching the mind scampering off, like the little monkey that it is, into the past, the future, anywhere but here, and suggests that the real skill in meditation is simply noticing that the mind has wandered. So liberating, this idea that we can start over at any time, a thousand times a day if need be. I see many parallels between the practices of meditation and writing but none are more powerful than this. Writing is hard. We resist, we procrastinate, we veer off course. But we have this tool, this ability to begin again. Every sentence is new. Every paragraph, every chapter, every book is a country we've never been to before. We're clearing brush. We don't know what's on the other side of that tree. We are visitors in a foreign land. And so we take a step. Up the stairs after the morning coffee. Back to the desk after the doorbell has rung. Return to the manuscript.

It never gets easier. It *shouldn't* get easier. Word after word, sentence after sentence, we build our writing lives. We hope not to repeat ourselves. We hope to evolve as interpreters and witnesses of the world around us. We feel our way through darkness, pause, consider, breathe in, breathe out, begin again. And again, and again.

Tics

I'm upstairs working when I hear a strange thumping sound coming from below, and I can't resist investigating. Any excuse to get up and stretch. I follow the sound to my dining room and catch sight of a blur of red slamming itself against the window. A cardinal is hurling itself at its own reflection in the glass. Does it think it's fighting another bird? Or mating? The poor thing keeps at it. *Slam.* Then back to the tree branch.

It must be dazed but it doesn't learn its lesson. *Slam*. Wings fluttering. Black eyes, black beak highlighted against the red. *Slam*. I want to help it but know I can't.

Things we do repeatedly are evidence of our own nature. These might be physical gestures: twirling hair, drumming fingers, biting nails. We might pour ourselves a glass of wine at six o'clock every evening. We might talk to ourselves or sing in the shower without even knowing it. We might have actual tics: a throbbing muscle under one eye, a shoulder that lifts involuntarily. When it comes to the writing life, we have these impulses, too. And—unlike our friend the cardinal—we can learn something about ourselves and our process if we pay close attention.

When I finished my novel *Black & White,* it had been through multiple drafts and close reads, but it wasn't until the book was in production that I received a note from a copy editor. "Do you realize," she wrote, "that the word *muffled* appears eleven times in this manuscript?" *Muffled.* The copy editor referenced the pages on which the offending word appeared. Sounds were muffled. Feelings were muffled. How had I not noticed? Muffled is not a word I use regularly in conversation. What had happened? How had I not caught this, in read after read?

The more I thought about it, the more I understood. And fortunately I still had time to do some small but important revisions—which didn't have to do simply with removing the *muffled*s, but rather, with realizing that each time I unconsciously repeated the word, I was not close enough to the interior life of my main character. She had been her mother's muse as a child—posing nude for a series of provocative photographs—an experience that continued to haunt and define her life as an adult. If you had asked me, while I was writing *Black & White,* if there were any direct autobiographical components to it, I would have told you no. But in fact I had been a child model myself. As a three-year-old, I was the Kodak poster child at Christmas, displayed on billboards all over America. And though the experience wasn't nearly as traumatic as the one I gave my main character, it was strange and confusing to be the Orthodox Jewish Christmas poster child. Those feelings were buried for me. *Muffled.* Those places in my manuscript—that unconscious repetition—were signals that I needed to dig a little deeper. What was being muffled? What was beneath that overused word?

Our tics are a road map to our most hidden and sensitive wounds. My husband has pointed out to me that when I describe my parents' car accident or Jacob's illness, I tend to fall back on the exact same language. *My father was killed, my mother had eighty broken bones. Rare seizure disorder; seven out of a million babies; only 15 percent survive.* I do this—and I would wager we all do—because I don't want to go back there.

I don't want to revisit the pain, and so I go on automatic pilot. *Eighty broken bones. Fifteen percent.* I prefer to skim the surface, hit the main points, and move on, thank you very much. But if we *are* interested in delving deeply, if we are students of the observed life, we'd best take a good hard look at these easy fallbacks. Repeated words. Familiar phrases. Consider them clues. When you discover them, slow down. In fact, stop. Become willing to press against the bruise—it's there anyway—and see what it yields.

STRUCTURE

I recently had a long phone conversation with a writer working on a first novel. This writer, a former journalist and television producer, had reached a low point. She was intensely frustrated by her lack of progress. I could hear it in her voice. She sounded strained, confused, almost angry at her book, as if it were a truculent child. Why wouldn't it behave? Structure was her problem, she told me. She had characters she loved and felt she knew well. She was halfway through the manuscript, and had outlined the rest of it, but now she found herself stuck.

At the word *outline,* I began to see a red flag waving. I had a feeling that I knew the problem. It is common among writers

113

who have been journalists, reporters, editors, business owners, attorneys, or pretty much any career that rewards concise and ordered thinking. It stands to reason, of course, that we ought to know where we're going before we set out—doesn't it? The outline serves as a literary form of a GPS. We wouldn't get into our car and head to an unfamiliar destination without plugging the address into our GPS, would we? We are comforted by that electronic voice—mine is a British woman who always sounds slightly miffed—telling us that our destination is ahead on the right.

Except that when it comes to creative writing—by which I mean the kind of work that the artist Anne Truitt describes as "the strict discipline of forcing oneself to work steadfastly along the nerve of one's own most intimate sensitivity"—outlines are not necessarily helpful. We need Doctorow's fog. If we know too much about where we're going, the work will suffer along the way. It will convulse and die before our eyes. We'll end up dragging along a corpse until finally, exhausted, we just give up.

Outlines offer us an illusion that we are in control, that we know where we're going. And while this may be comforting, it is also antithetical to the process of making work that lives and breathes. If we are painting by numbers, how can we give birth to something new? Jorie Graham also describes Mark Strand's poems on canvas in this way: "The columns swerve, making these abstract paintings, as in: what makes the shape move is the mind making mistakes, or taking change on, or trying out variations until the right one appears and stills the mind."

The mind making mistakes. This is what makes the shape move. Such a magnificent idea, and one to hold on to, that the mistakes themselves are what make the work alive. Structure may emerge in the middle, even may announce itself once we're in over our heads, in the thick of it, having relinquished control. Then, *then,* the architecture begins to whisper to us. We may have thought we were building a Gothic cathedral, only to find that the shape is an adobe. We may realize that our beginning is not the beginning at all, and that where we are, on page one hundred and sixty-five, is actually the starting point. We may realize that a minor character has taken over. That the book needs a prologue set fifty years before the story begins. It isn't always pleasant, when the true structure reveals itself, because it often means a lot more work. You may need to shore up the foundation, or perhaps you'll have to build an entirely new one.

My husband has a recurring fantasy in which he's a bricklayer. He finds something immensely satisfying in the idea of laying one brick at a time, not moving forward until that brick is cemented in place. He returns to this fantasy because it's the opposite of the writing process, which he likens to building a skyscraper in a swamp. You don't know—you *can't* know—whether the bricks you've laid on top will be supported by the bricks at the bottom. There's only one way to find out, and that is to build the thing, regardless.

"Maybe I should just throw my outline out the window," the fledgling novelist half-joked. I leapt. "Yes!" I nearly shouted into the phone, probably scaring her half to death. But then what, she wondered. Working with no signposts, no game plan is so frightening, such an anathema to most of us.

"Do you feel connected to your main characters?" I asked.

Yes, she told me. These characters were her whole reason for wanting to write the book. She was deeply invested in them and felt she had to tell their story.

I gave her, then, one of my favorite pieces of writing advice, from Aristotle's *Poetics*: "Action is not plot," wrote Aristotle, "but merely the result of pathos."

This is not just advice about writing, but about life itself, the whole megillah, the human catastrophe. If you have people, you will have pathos. We are incited by our feelings—by the love, rage, envy, sorrow, joy, longing, fear, passion—that lead us to action. Plot is really just a fancy word for whatever happens, and structure is a fancy word for how it happens. Plot can be as intricate as a whodunit, or as simple as a character experiencing a small but significant shift in perspective. But invariably it comes from the people we create on the page.

If you are creating something real, structure will reveal itself to you eventually. Look—there's the vista. You lay the bricks. Moments connect. History and heritage ripple through the present. A voice emerges like a strain of music. And then—through the fog—a shape. It may not be what you expected. It may not even be what you hoped for. But it will be yours.

CHANNEL

Agnes de Mille, who revolutionized musical theater by choreographing the dream ballet sequence in the 1943 Broadway hit *Oklahoma!*, confessed to her lifelong friend Martha Graham that she found the success of *Oklahoma!* strange and disheartening. She preferred her earlier dances, which had largely been ignored. She didn't think the ballet sequence was her best work by a long shot—only "fairly good." She went on to tell Graham that she had a burning desire to be excellent, but no faith that she could be.

Later, Graham told this to de Mille:

There is a vitality, a life force, a quickening that is translated through you into action. And because there is only one of you in all time, this expression is unique. If you block it, it will never exist through any other medium and be lost. The world will not hear it. It is not your business to determine how good it is; nor how valuable it is; nor how it compares with other expressions. It is your business to keep it yours, clearly and directly, to keep the channel open. You do not even need to believe in yourself or your work. You have to keep open and aware directly to the urges that motivate you. Keep the channel open. No artist is pleased. There is no satisfaction whatever at any time. There is only a queer, divine dissatisfaction, a blessed unrest that keeps us marching and makes us more alive than the others.

I have kept Martha Graham's advice tacked to the bulletin board above my desk for the past twenty years, and have returned again and again to the ideas it contains. *No satsifaction whatever at any time.* I find this bracing, honest, enormously comforting. Very possibly only a writer would find the notion of no satisfaction whatever at any time enormously comforting. But I do. It reminds me that I signed up for this, after all. I signed up for a life in which my job is to do my best possible work—to keep the channel open—while detaching myself from the end result. How I feel about my own work is none of my business. "We cannot achieve greatness unless we lose all interest in being great," wrote Thomas Merton. Satisfaction should not be—cannot be—the goal.

There is tremendous creative freedom to be found in letting go of our opinions of our work, in considering the possibility that we may not be our own best critic. As I sit here on the chaise longue in a ten-year-old ratty cardigan and my sweatpants, squinting through my reading glasses at my computer screen, as I plan the rest of my day (student work to be read, a book to review, a speech to write, a few small essays to think about) what I am struck by is the fullness of this, this writing life. My job is to *do,* not to judge. It is a great piece of luck, a privilege, to spend each day leaping, stumbling, leaping again. As is true of so much of life, it isn't what I thought it would be when I was first starting out. The price is high: the tension, isolation, and lack of certitude can sometimes wear me down. But then there is the aliveness. The queer, divine dissatisfaction. The blessed unrest.

SECOND ACTS

My husband and his screenwriter friends often talk about what they call "the second act problem." Another way of putting this would be the "middles" problem. Classic screenplay structure is broken into three acts. Act One builds on a brilliant premise. Act Three results in a startling conclusion. But the middle is all about the art of execution. How well do you know your characters? Do their actions reveal their interior lives? Does their behavior make emotional and psychological sense? Is the story moving forward, or bogging down? Middles demand form and consciousness. Otherwise, we risk falling into a baggy and bloated muddle of randomness.

Just as the middle of a life requires discernment and discipline, so does the middle of a story. We take a step back, we see where we are. We think about the shape we are making. Is it intentional? Or are we being buffetted by chance? This crafting of story—the honing of the muddle in the middle—can assume many forms. The classic narrative arc—a beginning followed by a slow and steady rise, culminating in an apex that then leads gracefully to an inevitable end—is only one of many tools at our disposal. As writers, we are able to play with time. So why not? Why don't we? We don't have to start at the beginning. We may want to start in the middle and retrace our steps backward. Or begin at the end and tell the rest of the story as prelude.

But we can only know this when we get there. We may make the painful discovery that our shiny premise has run out of steam. We may find out that the story we thought we were telling has changed on us in interesting and exciting ways. Whatever we find there marks the start of the real work of discovering our structure. The question of how we tell the story, how we structure the narrative so that it will tease out the inner workings of our characters' most intimate lives, of this pathos they find themselves experiencing at this particular moment, in this particular place—this *how,* which might seem mechanical, a question of rudimentary craft, is anything but. The narrative choices are endless. We can choose a single point of view or multiple points of view—a solo or a chorus. We can zoom way in and tell the story through the lens of one character, or pull back, use a wide angle, create an omniscient, God-like narrator. We can create a series of stories or chapters that only connect to one another glancingly, but to great effect, the way Joan Silber does in *Ideas of Heaven,* or as Jennifer Egan does in *A Visit From The Goon Squad,* or as does Michael Cunningham, who creates an operatic narrative out of three disparate characters' lives in *The Hours.*

But there are no shortcuts. We are often further along than we like when the true nature of a piece asserts itself. We have to toss out those fishing lines, follow their arcs, and see where they land. Then we have to sit there. It will quite possibly be a good long while before we know whether we've landed in Idaho's Salmon River—or in an unfortunate, mosquito-infested swamp.

At the risk of sounding like a Dr. Seuss story (the how and the who went out to play . . .) I mean to suggest that premises are lovely but—as anyone who has written themselves straight into a wall will tell you—middles are where you have to tough things out. Ideas fall apart. All that promise vanishes when facing the cold, harsh light of making something out of it. Middles challenge us to find our tenacity and our patience, to remind ourselves that it is within this struggle—often just at the height of hopelessness, frustration, and despair—that we find the most hidden and valuable gifts of the process. Just as in life.

ORDINARY LIFE

An infant's dire prognosis. A father's sudden death. A mother's broken bones. In a passage from Julian Barnes's novel *The Sense of an Ending,* a character considers the question of accumulation: "You put your money on a horse, it wins, and your winnings go on to the next horse in the next race, and so on. Your winnings accumulate. But do your losses? Not at the racetrack—there you just lose your original stake. But in life? Here, different rules apply. You bet on a relationship, it fails; you go on to the next relationship, it fails too: and maybe what you lose is not two simple minus sums but the multiple of what you staked. That's what it feels like, anyway. Life isn't just addition and subtraction. There's also accumulation, the multiplication of loss, of failure."

The two greatest shocks I have experienced—my parents' accident and my son's illness—ignited in me what had been an already flickering flame of awareness—some might even say a hyperawareness—that life is fragile. That bad things have happened and, without a doubt, will again. That to love anything at all is to become able to lose it. Some days, this awareness gets the better of me. Anxiety sets in. I grow impatient and controlling. Or I retreat from the world. But more often than not, this burden of accumulation feels like a gift. It has taught me that ordinary life—or what Joan Didion calls "ordinary blessings"—is what is most precious.

We are revealed to ourselves—just as our characters are revealed to us—through our daily actions. When making my son's breakfast, I try to focus simply on cracking the eggs, melting the butter, toasting the bread. It doesn't get more elemental than that. As I drive down country roads taking Jacob to school, I remind myself to focus on the way the sunlight plays on the surface of a pond, the silhouettes of cows in a field. I've learned that it isn't so easy to witness what is actually happening. The eggs, the cows. But my days are made up of these moments. If I dismiss the ordinary—waiting for the special, the extreme, the extraordinary to happen—I may just miss my life.

When I first started out, I thought that my characters and their circumstances had to be somehow *large*. I wrote a novel about a famous artist. Another about a psychoanalyst who had been through a public humiliation. I loved these characters, and they were real to me. But they weren't ordinary. When I turned to fiction again after writing my memoir *Slow Motion,* in the wake of Jacob's illness, it was an ordinary family that began to play around the edges of my mind. Perhaps I had come to see that life's greatest revelations are contained within the everyday. Virginia Woolf knew this. Her Mrs. Dalloway was a just a woman going about her business. It was her interior life that rendered Clarissa Dalloway extraordinary. Gustave Flaubert knew this. Emma and Charles Bovary were regular people trapped in a bind. Faulkner said that it is "the problem of the human heart in conflict with itself which alone can make good writing." The illuminating of that conflict—one that resides inside every heart still beating—is itself a thing of beauty because it allows the reader to experience empathy, oneness, identification. It allows that greatest consolation of literature, which is to pierce our separateness, to show us that, in this business of being human, we are not alone.

Marilynne Robinson, who in her novels *Housekeeping* and *Gilead* masterfully reveals the interior lives of characters who are at once ordinary and indelible, once said this in an interview with the *Paris Review*: "You have to have a certain detachment in order to see beauty for yourself rather than something that has been put in quotation marks to be understood as 'beauty.' Think about Dutch painting, where sunlight is falling on a basin of water and a woman is standing there in the clothes that she would wear when she wakes up in the morning—that beauty is a casual glimpse of something very ordinary. Or a painting like Rembrandt's *Carcass of Beef,* where a simple piece of meat caught his eye because there was something mysterious about it. You also get that in Edward Hopper: Look at the sunlight! Or look at the human being! These are instances of genius. Cultures cherish artists because they are people who can say, Look at that. And it's not Versailles. It's a brick wall with a ray of sunlight falling on it."

It is the job of the writer to say, *look at that.* To point. To shine a light. But it isn't that which is already bright and beckoning that needs our attention. We develop our sensitivity—to use John Berger's phrase, our "ways of seeing"—in order to bear witness to *what is.* Our tender hopes and dreams, our joy, frailty, grief, fear, longing, desire—every human being is a landscape. The empathic imagination glimpses the woman working the cash register at a convenience store, the man coming out of the bathroom at the truck stop, the mother chasing her toddler up and down the aisle of the airplane, and knows what it sees. *Look at that.* This human catastrophe, this accumulation of ordinary blessings, of unbearable losses. And still, a ray of sunlight, a woman doing the wash, a carcass of beef. The life that holds us. The life we know.

SECRETS

When we speak of a character's inner life, we are talking about what is thought but left unsaid. What motivates action but remains hidden—perhaps even from the character herself. Perhaps even—quite possibly even—from the *writer* herself, at least when first discovering the story on the page. We don't know our characters all that well when we start out. Even if we've compiled complete dossiers, even if we've written whole family trees, still, we discover our characters' obsessions, their secret shame, their hidden guilt, their base desires, their most private longings, as we go along. We can't possibly know that when we begin. And so it's in the middle—just as is true of our own lives—that we make some of our most stirring discoveries.

In her essay on writing, "Outlaw Heart," Jayne Anne Phillips asks the question: "Which of us become writers, and why?" If it were possible to trace the roots of any writing life back to its very inception, to the seeds, to the tender shoots deep within the fertile ground, we would inevitably find ourselves in the territory of childhood. If we write in order to make sense of the world around us, where else but in childhood does this need to know, to understand, take hold? Sometimes my husband and I are in the midst of a conversation in hushed tones about some grown-up matter—a friend's divorce, a betrayal, a financial concern, another friend's miscarriage—when suddenly our son tunes in from the other room where we had thought he was busy doing homework.

What? He calls out to us. *What are you talking about?*

Nothing, we respond.

No, really—what?

Grown-up stuff. And if forced, our tempers short: *None of your business.*

In her essay, Phillips writes about her novel *Shelter,* in which the characters are children. "It has its genesis in my childhood self, not in what happened to me, but in how I thought, in the nameless implications I perceived and the echoes of those implications, heard for years. There were secrets, and somehow those secrets became my responsibility." Phillips goes on to write that "we children who become writers evolve into a particular genus of angelic spy, absorbing information, bargaining with ourselves, banking on the possibility that we might someday intervene in the dynamics of loss, insist that sorrow will not be meaningless."

Whether war reportage or childhood memoir, a sprawling family saga or the slimmest and most elliptical of stories, we are that child, straining to hear. We have taken in way more than we know, more than we understand, and we write in order to find out: What's true? What happened? How can it be? And what can be done?

Our parents often want to shield us from their own heartaches, their own histories, for as long as they possibly can. I didn't need to know about my mother's first failed marriage, or my father's loss of his beautiful young bride, or my uncle's suicide attempt, or my aunt's mental collapse. I didn't need to know about them, but I absorbed them anyway. I overheard, I snooped, I intuited. My parents tried to protect me, but to be a parent is ultimately to fail to protect. Just recently, a mother of one of my son's classmates was diagnosed with a terminal illness. Our boy and his friends will have a front-row seat to the stark fact of premature loss. As much as I don't believe in secrets, I, too, stumble when relaying some hard bit of information to my son. I don't like using words like *heart attack, cancer, divorce, terrorism, prison, war, death*. I don't like to use them, but to omit them from my vocabulary is to create a redacted document—the black bits stand out.

Whether an overheard whisper or a gruesome story comes across on the nightly news, we angelic spies live out our childhoods with a knowledge growing inside of us, spreading like moss in a dark place. When we become writers, we are driven by the echoes of those implications—of what we feel and intuit but cannot know. As we set our stories down on the page, our inner life becomes the only tool we have with which to reenter that dark place. Our eyes adjust. We don't see everything. Phillips writes that we "live in the dim or glorious shadows of partially apprehended shapes." We mine the secret life, our responsibility. We make it our business.

PRACTICE

I wrote my first novel in that small, borrowed room down the hall from my apartment on the Upper West Side. My second novel was written in a modern high-rise on the Upper East Side when I was parched, lonely, and briefly married to the wrong person. I wrote my third novel in a series of apartments and in a house in Sag Harbor, deeply absorbed in my work, with only my Yorkshire Terrier for company. I met my husband when I was just a few chapters into my first memoir. I remember giving him a piece of it to read one weekend, and lying in bed in a cottage near the beach, listening to the pages rustle in the next room, anxious about what he would think. By the time I wrote my next novel, I was a mother—a frightened one in the wake of Jacob's illness. I began that book in our Brooklyn brownstone, and revised it once we'd moved to rural Connecticut. My books since then have all been composed in that same Connecticut countryside. The meadows. The stone walls. The dogs. The quiet.

When we first moved to our house in the country—a house that prompts visitors to inquire where we buy food, whether Jacob has any other kids to play with, and what on earth we *do* all day—our friends were taking bets. *Oh, you'll be back,* they said. We were urban creatures, after all. When we first moved into our house, I didn't like being alone. It felt strange, isolating, even dangerous. Scenes from Stephen King novels and Brian De Palma films played out in my head. I imagined midnight break-ins and bears clawing through cans in the garage. I woke up each morning to stillness. Silence. In New York, the world was a rushing stream. If I wasn't sure what to do, the city supplied plenty of ideas. I could be carried along by the momentum of that current—decisionless, actionless, but in motion.

In the country, when I opened the front door, the only signs of life were a bluebird, a hawk circling overhead, a white-tailed deer, the occasional fox. I was left with myself, and I hardly knew what to do. The hours would take on no shape unless I shaped them. I had managed to have a routine for all of my writing years prior to moving to the country—I had written four books that way—but I began to see that it had been a series of habits strung together. Not a practice.

Practice involves discipline but is more closely related to patience. I was nearly forty years old when we left the city, and I had mastered a series of skills that allowed me to be productive. I knew how to find a good café in which to work. I avoided meeting friends for lunch (or, god forbid, breakfast) because it disrupted my writing day. I knew how to wear earphones to tune out the sound of jackhammers on the street below. But in the sudden absence of cafés, noise, or nearby friends, my old habits no longer served me. I had to rethink everything. Surrounded by nothing but space and silence, I saw that up until then, I had been *reacting* to the ready distractions of city life, like a spinning top, the slightest bump against anything—a person, a red light, a shop window—and off I might go in another direction. Yes, I got my work done. But at what cost?

One of the cornerstones of Buddhist philosophy is the notion of dharma—the Sanskrit word that, loosely translated, means teaching, or wisdom, or life's path. Practice is about engagement with one's own dharma. The articulation, the expression, day after day after day, of our truest selves. Writing, it seems to me, is dharma practice. If we are patient, if we place ourselves in the path of possibility, we just might find our own rushing current—more powerful than that of any city street.

Lives are made up of days. Days, made up of hours, of minutes, of seconds during which we make choices, and those choices can become practice. When it comes to the practice of writing, it cannot be distraction that propels us but rather the patience—the openness, the willingness—to meet ourselves on the page. To stop being at the mercy of what we surround ourselves with, but rather, to discover our story.

"Practice," said the great yogi Pattabhi Jois to the students gathered at his shala in Mysore, India. He was eighty, maybe even ninety years old and I am certain he was speaking as much to himself as to them, as good teachers always do. "Practice and all is coming."

INHERITANCE

My father is buried in a massive Brooklyn cemetery where wild dogs roam in the night and the elevated train rumbles overhead. I get lost each time I visit his grave, and wander among tombstones until I find it. He is surrounded by his grandparents, his parents, a brother, a few cousins. His second wife is buried in her own family's plot, a few hundred steps away. It was startling when I came upon her headstone: the dates bracketing her brief life, just beneath her surname, *Shapiro*. My father's first wife is buried somewhere in New Jersey. I remember attending the funeral with my half-sister. His third wife—my mother—is also buried in New Jersey, down by the shore, near the chicken farm where she grew up. She is buried in *her* family's plot. When she was dying, my mother made it clear that she did not wish to end up in the Brooklyn cemetery; she did not want to spend eternity with *those* people, the ones she had disliked with passion for more than forty years. *I feel sorry for you,* my mother said from her deathbed, eyes gleaming. *You'll have to visit your parents in two different cemeteries.*

In my basement, on the other side of the wall from Jacob's playroom (piano, ukelele, bean bag chairs, and half-finished board games scattered across the floor) I have the detritus of my family's life. It's all just thrown in there in a jumble. Most boxes have remained unopened for these nearly ten years since my mother's death. Some are labelled in her hand: "Peru," or "delicate," or "important papers!" Her wedding dress—ankle-length ice-blue tulle with a French lace bodice, the height of fashion for a second wedding in 1957—is not packed in mothballs as it should be but, rather, is tossed across a bench next to our wine cellar as if waiting for the ghost of my young, glamorous mother to come along and dance in it once more. Also in this mess—which my husband keeps suggesting we tackle on some rainy weekend—are my childless aunt's fifty-year-old golf clubs, my uncle's framed medical diploma and a basketball signed to him by the NCAA-winning Rutgers basketball players, for whom he was team physician.

"Where does the pain go?" asks Donna Masini in her poem "Eye of the Skull." The poet has come from the dentist, where she's just had a cavity filled. She walks down the street, her mouth numb, when she notices a crazy woman behind her. "An older woman / dressed as a young girl. She had gone to a good school / liked good things. Had had them too. You could tell. / She is screaming into herself, into the air. Vulgar things, shouting them to no one in particular / that I can see."

I remember reading this poem with a shock of recognition. It was shortly after a spate of losses: my father, grandmother, and two uncles, all within a year. My mother was living in a rehabilitation center. My remaining relatives had stopped speaking to each other. Bad blood boiled to the surface. My relationship had ended. I read Masini's poem and identified with both the numb poet and the crazy woman. I knew the pain went somewhere—I was quaking from it—and also afraid of it. I was afraid that if I let myself fully feel the accumulation of those losses, the enormity of them, I would become the crazy woman. I would go to a place from which I'd never be able to recover, to return. "What is trapped in the bones, the gearlike teeth / that join the two fused cramped parts / of the skull? What clenches and curls in the marrow? / Did the pain surface, just then? Did all that / numbed pain come in one great rush?"

I needn't have worried. To write is to have an ongoing dialogue with your own pain. To scream to it, with it, from it. To know it—to know it cold. Whether you're writing a biography of Abraham Lincoln, a philosophical treatise, or a work of fiction, you are facing your demons *because they are there*. To be alone in a room with yourself and the contents of your mind is, in effect, to go to that place, whether you intend to or not. I recently met a writer who is also a psychoanalyst. She laughingly recounted a conversation at a dinner party, in which she told the man seated next to her that she was doing postdoctoral training in trauma. "You *want* to do that?" he asked her, baffled that anyone would choose to do such a thing.

Just as I know that a holy mess waits for me on the other side of the wall from Jacob's playroom, I also know that it's only a representation (all that stuff!) of the holy mess inside of me. The ghost of my mother who died confused and angry. The ghost of my father who I still talk to every day. The golf clubs and medical diplomas of aunts and uncles left in the hands of the last person for whom it will have any meaning. *What clenches and curls in the marrow.*

The mess *is* holy. What we inherit—and how we come to understand what we inherit—is all we have to work with. There is beauty in *what is*. Every day, when I sit down to work, I travel to that place. Not because I'm a masochist. Not because I live in the past. But because my words are my pickax, and with them I chip away at the rough surface of whatever it is I still need to know.

Not Always So

The Buddhist teacher Jack Kornfield once said that all of life can be summed up in these three words: *not always so*. We plan on our day going in a certain direction? Not always so. We expect a friend or relative to behave the way they always have? Not always so. There is the pattern, and then there is the dropped stitch that disrupts the pattern, making it all the more complex and interesting.

Stories are about the dropped stitch. About what happens when the pattern breaks. Though there is a certain poetry in the rhythm of the everyday, it is most often a shift, a moment of not-always-so, that ends up being the story. Why is this moment different? What has changed? And why now? We would do well to ask ourselves these questions when we're at work. This shift can be a massive one (here I am thinking of the dystopian novel in which the very rhythms of the universe are called into question: the sun no longer predictably rises in the east or sets in the west; a meteor is hurling toward earth; the oceans are rising), or it can be as subtle and internal as the

Steven Millhauser story, "Getting Closer," in which a nine-year-old boy on vacation with his family feels, for the first time, a searing, wordless awareness of time's passage.

Why are we writing about this moment, and no other? And what can we do—stylistically, structurally, linguistically—to get inside it? How can we reveal the innards, the pulsing truth of this character who is—let's face it—at some sort of juncture, because if he isn't, why would the story be worth telling? The Millhauser story takes place within the span of just a few minutes. It unpacks, layer after layer, the dawning consciousness of its nine-year-old protagonist. The action of the story, so to speak, involves the boy dipping his toe into the water for the first time that summer. That—in terms of external action, in terms of plot—is it. Nothing else happens. Can you imagine Millhauser having to answer the question, *What are you working on?* while he was writing that story?

But what goes on internally in "Getting Closer" is gripping to the point of leaving the reader breathless. We are guided deep into the inner world of that boy, tracing thought after thought until we *are* him, we become him, and this is literature doing its job, which is to penetrate the surface, to dismantle the ordinary, to find the dropped stitch, to show us that we are—all of us—built of these not-always-so moments, that they mark the turning points of our lives.

GRAVY

I am on the chaise longue, cross-legged, my computer nestled into a cushion on my lap. It's my best time to be writing—first thing in the morning, before I'm distracted by those "fleas of life." The house is empty. There is nothing stopping me from getting to work. Except that I can feel it: a restlessness, an unease. I'm about to get in my own way. The Internet beckons. The book review due next week feels suddenly pressing. The galleys and manuscripts piled across my office are calling my name. The previous night's dreams hover just at the edges of my consciousness, throwing me off balance.

It's so easy to forget what matters. When I begin the day centered, with equanimity, I find that I am quite unshakable. But if I start off in that slippery, discomfiting way, I am easily thrown off course—and once off course, there I stay. And so I know that my job is to cultivate a mind that catches itself. A mind that watches its own desire to scamper off into the bramble, but instead, guides itself gently back to what needs to be done. This kind of equanimity may not be my nature, but I can at least attempt to make it my habit. I was a young writer when I first read Donald Hall's memoir, *Life Work,* but

I still remember the way he described a "best day" spent on the New Hampshire farm he inherited from his grandparents: "This morning, when I have worked over as much prose as I wish to, when I feel tired, it's 10:00 A.M. I've been up five and a half hours, and over the last four hours I have done my day's work. It's 10:00 A.M and the rest of the day is gravy."

Hall goes on to describe the rest of this ideal day's activities—this gravy—in great detail: he dictates the changes he's made to his manuscript, gathers the tapes of letters he dictated while watching the previous night's Red Sox game, and delivers it all to his (yes) typist. He shaves. Reads a friend's manuscript. Proofreads an index. Now it's time for lunch. He takes a nap with his wife, the poet Jane Kenyon, and—he matter-of-factly lets us know—they have sex. Then he takes his dog for a long walk. Comes home, reads the day's mail (letters from old friends and acquaintances, and requests and invitations, most of which he politely declines). Maybe he does an errand or two—nothing taxing, just the grocery store or filling up the car with gas—and then he picks up the clean pages from his typist and it's back to work for a few more hours. The day ends with dinner and another Red Sox game, during which he flosses his teeth and again dictates letters.

A stunning example of a writer who accepts and understands that his work is the only thing that will save him. His tone is the same throughout, focused—gently, quietly, but unshakably, it seems—on the task at hand. He is a writer who (at least on the best day) does not succumb to inner or outer pressure but, rather, knows that what he calls "absorbedness" is the answer—the only answer. Through all of life's twists and turns—those fleas—he turns to work the way his grandparents turned to the soil, to the harvest, which waits for no one. He operates with a tempered sense of urgency. His daughter gives birth; his elderly mother falls ill; he is diagnosed with a tumor in his liver; his wife—we know, reading this book years after it was written—his wife will die tragically young, of leukemia. Still, there is this day, and there is work to be done. This absorbedness does not come from a cold heart—no, quite the opposite. It is a hedge against mortality, against depression, against indignity, against misfortune, against paralyzing sorrow. It is not a magic pill but, rather, a stark fact. After his own cancer diagnosis, Hall writes: "If work is no antidote to death, nor a denial of it, death is a powerful stimulus to work. *Get done what you can.*" There is this—only this. It would be good to keep these words in mind when we wake up each morning. *Get done what you can.* And then, the rest is gravy.

The Cave

I once heard this story from a friend of Joyce Carol Oates. The writer was sitting at the breakfast table at home in Princeton with her husband, Ray Smith. Ray was reading the paper when he happened upon a review of Joyce's new novel. He asked if she wanted to see it.

"No," she replied.

No?

"If it's a good review it will ruin my writing day, and if it's a bad review, it will ruin my writing day. Either way, I intend to have a writing day."

I don't know whether this story is true but I like it anyway. The understanding that *excitement*—whether the happy kind or not—will make the work all but impossible. It gets a person revved up. And a revved up state is not useful. A writer in the midst of a piece of work might do well to think of herself as nineteenth-century neurasthenic: frail and easily startled, best off bundled in a blanket with a cup of tea, in a lawn chair, perhaps, gazing out from Magic Mountain.

I like excitement as much as the next person. Perhaps even more than the next person. But I get overstimulated easily, and

I can feel my brain shorting out when I have too much going on. And it doesn't take much: a good piece of news, a nice review, a longed-for assignment, a cool invitation, and suddenly I can't think straight. The outside world glitters, it gleams like a shiny new toy. Squinting, having lost all sense of myself, I toddle with about as much consciousness as a two-year-old in the direction of that toy. Once I get a little bit of it, I am conditioned to want more, more, more. I lose all sight of whatever I had been doing before.

One of the strangest aspects of a writing life is what I think of as *going in and out of the cave.* When we are in the middle of a piece of work, the cave is the only place we belong. Yes, there are practical considerations. Eating, for instance. Or helping a child with homework. Or taking out the trash. Whatever. But a writer in the midst of a story needs to find a way to keep her head there. She can't just pop out of the cave, have some fun, go dancing, and then pop back in. The work demands our full attention, our deepest concentration, our best selves. If we're in the middle—in the boat we're building—we cannot let ourselves be distracted by the bright and shiny. The bright and shiny is a mirage, an illusion. It is of no use to us.

If there is a time for that brightness, it is at the end: when the book is finished and the revisions have been turned in, when you've given everything inside of you and then some. When the cave is empty. Every rock turned over. The walls covered with hieroglyphics that only you understand—notes you've written to yourself in the darkness. But it's possible that something interesting has happened while you've toiled amid the moths and millipedes. Once you've acclimated to cave life, stumbling toward the light may have lost some of its appeal. What glitters looks shopworn. The sparkle and hum of life outside the cave feels somehow less real than what has taken place deep within its recesses. Savor it—this hermetic joy, this rich, unexpected peace. It's hard-won, and so easy to lose. It contains within it the greatest contentment I have ever known.

CONTROL

"I was working on the proof of one of my poems all morning, and took out a comma," wrote Oscar Wilde. "In the afternoon, I put it back again." Let's face it: most of us are perfectionists. We spend our days searching for the perfect turn of phrase. And we consider this a good time. Who else would care so much about getting it right? Who else would need the silence, the uninterrupted stretches of time, the special mug, the favorite pen? We ponder each word, aim high, strive for both music and meaning. We know that one is nothing without the other. But we are not in control, and perhaps the silence, solitude, mug, and pen are our way of dealing with the fact that we are not masters of any universe—not even the universe of our own creation. Annie Dillard refers to this lack of control as a structural mystery: "Sometimes part of a book simply gets up and walks away. The writer cannot force it back in place. It wanders off to die."

We can't know when this is going to happen; when a book or a story is going to just up and change on us. If we are creating a living, genuine work of art—if we are approaching it with creativity and openness—this not only can, but *will* happen. The structural mystery Dillard writes about is a part of the process. So how do we make peace with the knowledge that every word, every sentence we write may very well hit the cutting room floor? Well, we don't make peace with this knowledge. We willfully disregard it. We find the rhythm of our process—the dance between knowing and not knowing—and we discover, along the way, how best to see the work clearly for what it is.

There are those writers who need to lay it all out, as fast as they possibly can, very possibly not in order, very often by hand, scribbling, scribbling, gaining as much access to their unconscious mind as they can by letting it loose on the page without self-editing. Some of my friends who work like this refer to it as vomiting. I'd prefer to find a more elegant term for it, but I'm not sure I can. Maybe I'm envious. This is not the kind of writer I am. I'm guessing that the vomiters are also people who can wake up in the morning and leave home with their beds unmade and dishes piled in the sink. Me, I'm not built that way. I make my bed first thing. Pillows fluffed. Hospital corners. And if I were to try to leave the house with a sinkful of dishes, I'd probably spend the day twitching. Which is to say, I am a compulsive, orderly person and my method of working reflects this. I inch forward, a sentence at a time. I read a few paragraphs back, then move forward only when I'm satisfied. Of course, I may be satisfied with a mirage. I may find—months later—that I'll have to scrap a whole passage, or chapter, or worse. But in the moment, I am making the prose shine, burnishing each word.

There are as many intricacies to the process as there are writers struggling to find their way. It's a matter of discovering what works for you, and eliminating the *shoulds*. My husband will often leap forward and write a scene that he thinks will appear later in a screenplay, because it has come to him in that moment. I could never do this. I need to write linearly, even when the work itself is not linear. I put one foot in front of the other. He pole-vaults from beginning to middle to end and back again, assembling the pieces as they come. He's also able to work in the middle of the night. My brain shuts off when the sun goes down. I have never worked well at night, prefering the daylight hours when I feel comforted by the knowledge that other people are awake all around me. The vomiters (okay, let's call them scribblers) feel in control when they are blasting through a story, finding shape as they go. The leapfroggers, like my husband, feel in control when they follow their spontaneous instincts. And me—I polish as I go. This gives me the illusion of control even as I, in the same breath, relinquish it.

READING YOURSELF

One of the great paradoxes of the writing life is that our words—chosen carefully, so thoughtfully, with deep focus and dedication—those words once on the page go dead on us. Language is ours only when we are forming sentences, moving elements around, grappling with punctuation, speaking words aloud, feeling them on our lips. While we are shaping a scene into something we can hear and touch and see, that scene lives and breathes. We are inside language like painters, we are working in our medium: the tempera, the thin line, the wet oil on canvas, still in process, still alive.

But once we commit—once those words dry like paint, are affixed to the page—it becomes nearly impossible to see them. *This?* We think to ourselves. Our most loathsome critic emerges with a swirl of her cape. *Really? What the hell is this?* The sentences appear to have been written in another language—a dark dream language, tucked into some musty, inaccessible corner of our psyche. Attempting to discern its meaning is a bit like looking at our own face in the mirror. It is at once so familiar as to be invisible, and so intimate that we turn away, baffled, ashamed.

Can we ever see ourselves, really? Can we read ourselves?

It is a powerful conundrum because without the ability to see our writing afresh we cannot do the necessary work. How do we know whether a problem lies with the work, or with our inability to enter it? We need clarity, but not coldness. Openness, but not attachment. We want optimism, but that optimism must go hand in hand with discernment. We're not looking for a cheerleader, nor a fault-finding judge. We want to read ourselves with equanimity.

How can we do this? Over the years, I've tried everything in an attempt to teach myself how to approach my own work. I've carried pages with me, and read them in unfamiliar settings, at odd hours, by candlelight, or at the beach, or on the subway, in an attempt to break my usual reading habits. I've changed the font on a manuscript: Garamond versus Times New Roman. I've poured myself a glass of wine at the end of a long writing day and sat quietly, pages and red pencil in hand. And while all of these can sometimes be effective (that is, if one glass of wine doesn't lead to another and another) my best, most secret weapon is this: *I pretend to be someone else.*

But that "someone else" can't be just anybody. Just as in choosing other readers for your work, when you're deciding who to pretend to be, it is important to choose with care. You're looking for someone kind but honest. Smart. And inclined to be interested in the world you're exploring. You would not, for instance, choose as a pretend-reader of your science fiction novel, someone who finds H. G. Wells insufferable and has never watched an episode of *Star Trek*. You need a pretend-reader whose criticism will be motivated by genuine interest, generosity of spirit, and literary acumen. Someone beneficent and wise.

If you're doubtful about this method, think about what happens right after you've sent a story, an essay, a manuscript, out to someone for a read. Perhaps you've submitted it to a literary magazine, or sent a draft to your editor. Doesn't it always happen that as soon as you've sent it, suddenly you notice something you want to change? You read your own work differently once you've shared it because you are—in that moment after you've hit the *send* button, or stuffed that envelope into the mail slot—rereading your work *as the person to whom you've just sent it.* The circle around your work suddenly grows wider. But now that you have a little more room in which to read it clearly, you've sent it out. It's too late.

So instead, find a quiet spot. Sit for a few moments with your manuscript in front of you. Close your eyes and become this other person, the way an actor inhabits a role. Ready? When you open your eyes the words in front of you will no longer be your own. They will be alive, mutable, and new. You are no longer yourself—in all your intimate fallibility—reading your own chicken scratch. Instead, you are a lucid, kind-hearted stranger—open to the possibilities. You are someone else: optimistic and ready to be surprised.

Dumb

We can have high IQs and all sorts of impressive degrees. Some of us can conjugate verbs in three languages, or understand particle physics. Maybe we went to Ivy League schools, or are members of Mensa. But being wicked smart won't help you when you're following a line of words on the page. In fact, being that kind of smart can turn out to be a problem. I know a few writers—intellectual, erudite people—whose work suffers for their brilliance. Though there is no such thing as too smart to be, say, a rocket scientist or a neurosurgeon, it is indeed possible to be too smart to be a writer.

When it comes to storytelling (and it's *all* storytelling) I often tell my students that we need to be dumb like animals. Storytelling iself is primal. It's the way we've always come to understand the world around us—whether recited around a campfire, or read aloud in an East Village bar. And so it stands to reason that in order to tell our stories, we tap into something beyond the intellect—an understanding deeper than anything we can willfully engage. Overthink and our minds scramble, wondering: Should we go in this direction? Or that one? Words can become so tangled that our process can feel more like an attempt to unravel the mess we've already made. We create obstacles, then strain to get around them. Our minds spin webs that obscure the light. We second-guess. We become lost in the morass of our limited consciousness.

But when we *feel* our way through a story, we are following a deep internal logic. The words precede us. We hear them. We sense their rightness. *How did I do that,* we ask ourselves, once we've finished, once the paint has dried, once we've worked through draft after draft after draft. Of course, part of the answer is that we've worked hard. We've kept ourselves in the chair. We've created an environment in which we can focus. We've read and researched and learned and explored. But there is something else—something we can't explain, and can't understand, and that makes us all feel a little bit like maybe we're cheating, except that it isn't cheating, it is the thing itself. *How did I do that?*

We are animals, our ears pricked, our eyes wide open. We put one hoof down, then another, on the soft and pliant earth. The rustle of a leaf. The crack of a branch. A passing breeze. We do not stop to ponder, *What's around the corner?* We don't know. There is only this: the bird's nest, the fawn, the snake curled beneath the gnarled root of an ancient tree. There is only the sound of our own breath. Our pulsing bodies. We are here. Alive, alert, quivering. We are cave dwellers. With a sharpened arrowhead we make a picture. A boy. A bear. The moon.

BREAKING THE RULES

Inevitably, I will be in the midst of giving my students some basic, creative-writing-101 type of advice (use adverbs sparingly, keep exclamation points to a minimum, ditto for ellipses) and they will diligently (whoops, an adverb) hunch over their notebooks, scribble down my words as if they're the gospel, and I will begin reeling off examples of books I love that break those rules. When Andrew Sean Greer wrote *The Confessions of Max Tivoli,* in which his narrator grew younger and younger with each passing chapter, he wasn't adhering to conventions of narrative structure. When Marion Winik wrote her tiny, exquisite memoir, *The Glen Rock Book of the Dead,* a jigsaw of elegies to people she had known who had passed away, she was breaking rules. Everyone's dead? Then why should we care? When Joe Brainard wrote *I Remember,* a memoir in which every sentence begins with those words, *I remember,* he didn't have the voice of some writing teacher in his head, suggesting that he avoid repetition. And when Colum McCann composed *Let the Great World Spin,* he didn't ask whether readers would be willing to follow the story lines of his multiple narrators until the threads connected. No. If any one of these writers had allowed their inner censor to swoop in, they may not have written those books. And the world wouldn't have them.

My favorite recent works of literature take risks. Unpredictable, unexpected, populated by characters who do the wrong thing, not according to plan. The plan pretty much never goes accordingly in life. Why should it, in literature? Give me a spectacular mess of a novel any day over an overly careful one. Give me kinetic prose, or deeply flawed, complex characters who surprise me. Give me sentences that go on for pages, leaving me breathless. Or, in the case of Jennifer Egan's *A Visit From the Goon Squad,* a chapter written in the form of a PowerPoint presentation. Or a series of blank pages, like those we come across in *When Women Were Birds,* Terry Tempest Williams's meditation on the journals her terminally ill mother asked that she read only after her death; journals, it turned out, that were themselves blank. When we reach that first blank page, when we turn it to find another, then another, we enter Tempest Williams's experience of what it must have been like to encounter her mother's empty journals. It's a breathtaking moment—and a bold one.

These instances of creative daring are moments of grace. They are moments when we get out of our own way. They break the rules, and break them beautifully. They arrive with no fanfare, but there is no mistaking them. They glide past our hesitation, our resistance, layers of reasons why we can't, we musn't, we shouldn't. They are accompanied by an almost childlike thrill. *Why not,* the whole universe seems to whisper: Why not now? Why not you? What's the worst thing that can happen?

Of course, maybe it won't work. Maybe the blank pages, the PowerPoint, the repetition—whatever the impossible thing you're doing—will fall flat. But if you don't embrace the danger of it, that knife's edge, that exquisite question—can it be done?—you will never know the pleasure that comes with throwing all those workshop rules, along with your copy of Strunk and White, out the window. You—and consequently we—will never know what could have been.

SPIT

At a recent Kundalini yoga class, the teacher asked the assembled group to do a breathing exercise. We all cupped our hands, making small bowls beneath our chins, and then . . . then we spit. We inhaled, then spit. Inhaled, then spit. For what seemed an interminable time but was probably five minutes, we inhaled, then spit. The teacher instructed us to dredge up every single painful thing we could from the recesses of our memory. Every bit of grief, regret, shame, guilt. "This is going to be messy," she said. "But I promise—nobody's watching."

A few dozen of us sat on our mats on the floor of the meeting house, the late afternoon sun streaming in through the west-facing windows. Chins wet with drool. Cupped hands slimy and damp. The room filled with the deeply strange and disconcerting sound of communal spitting. "Don't stop!" the teacher urged. She was an improbably beautiful, serene-looking blonde woman who was dressed for class in head-to-toe white. "Whatever you do, don't stop!"

Spit, spit, spit. I felt sick after a while. Nauseated. I kept my gaze trained on my cupped hands. Grief, regret, shame, and guilt pooled there. I saw my mother in my hands, not as the vibrant woman she was for my whole life, but as the frail, balding, tufted creature she became in the months before she died. *Spit, spit.* I saw my father, lying in a coma in the ICU after the car accident. *Spit.* I saw my half-sister from whom I am hopelessly estranged, her expression quizzical and dismissive. *Spit.* My son as an infant having seizures. *Spit.* Every funeral I've ever been to. *Spit.* The married man I slept with. *Spit.* The friend I betrayed. *Spit.*

"Thirty more seconds!" the teacher called out. It felt impossible to keep going. Was I the only one who felt this way? I resisted the urge to take a look around the room. When she finally, mercifully, told us to stop, my stomach was churning. The room seemed to be tilted. I felt simultaneously sickened and cleansed, my insides scoured raw.

What clenches and curls in the marrow. Why would any sane person put herself through such an exercise? For that matter, why meditation, why therapy, why all the endless self-scrutiny? A room full of people spitting, for gods sake! Aren't there better things to do on a sunny afternoon? But somehow—though the whole thing was embarrassing and didn't feel exactly good—I had the sense that what I was doing was, as my writer friends and I sometimes say, good for the work.

"Know your own bone," Thoreau wrote. "Gnaw at it, bury it, unearth it, gnaw it still." Of course, the beginning of this powerful piece of wisdom is: "Do what you love." In order to do what we love—whether we are woodworkers, legal-aid attorneys, emergency room physicians, or novelists—we must first know ourselves as deeply as we are able. *Know your own bone.* This self-knowledge can be messy. *Spit, spit.* But it is at the center of our life's work, this gnawing, this unearthing. There is never an end to it. Our deepest stories—our bones—are our best teachers. *Gnaw it still.*

CIGARETTE BREAK

Back when I smoked, whenever I got stuck midsentence, or needed a breather, I reached for my pack of Marlboro Reds. That pack of cigarettes was never far from me. I kept it near my right elbow, on my desk next to a ceramic ashtray swiped from the Hotel du Cap-Eden-Roc in Cap d'Antibes. That ashtray was pretty much always overflowing with butts. In my borrowed room on West Seventy-second Street, I wrote and smoked. Smoked and wrote. The two seemed linked together in a way that did not allow for the possibility that I would ever be able to write without the option of smoking. What would I do when I hit a snag? How could I possibly unstick myself without the ritual of tapping a cigarette loose from the pack, placing it between my lips, striking a match, lighting it . . . the tip glowing red? Without blowing out the match, leaning back in my desk chair, inhaling, exhaling, aiming smoke rings at the ceiling? Even as I write this, more than twenty years after my last cigarette, I can feel the welcome harshness of the smoke in my lungs, the feel of the cigarette between the second and third finger of my right hand.

By the time I had finished a draft of my first novel, I had quit smoking. My father had died, my mother was in a wheelchair. One afternoon, a tiny Yorkshire terrier puppy in the window of a pet store on Columbus Avenue caught my eye. I went inside, telling myself I was just going to play with him. An hour later, I left the pet store with a crate, puppy food, bowls, a leash, a collar, and a puppy. I named him Gus—Gustave, because I was reading a lot of Flaubert at the time—and every morning I took him to Central Park. One morning, as I sat on a rock warmed by the sunshine, smoking while Gus romped in the grass, the words *I want to live* went through my head and I stubbed out what would turn out to be my last cigarette. *I want to live.*

But when I went back to work on a second draft of that novel—now no longer a smoker—I was in trouble. I wanted to live, but I also needed to write. Those cigarette breaks had provided me with a ritualized dream time. Smoking was good for the writing. That tapping of the pack, lighting of the match, leaning back, and smoking, allowed for a prescribed amount of time—three minutes? five?—in which I was doing nothing but smoking, gazing out the window at the courtyard below, and allowing my thoughts to sort themselves out.

Writers require that ritualized dream time. We all have our tricks and tools. Some of us still smoke. I have friends who chew on pens. Or doodle. Friends who pop jelly beans from jars on their desks. Or take baths in the middle of the day. My husband and I recently discovered the power of pistachio nuts: the cracking open of those shells is curiously satisfying. Whatever keeps us in the work, engaged, and able to resist the urge to go do something—anything—else.

As I sit here writing this—at a café not far from my house—that urge is part of nearly every minute. Discomfort is kicking my ass on this particular day. I know better—but knowing better sometimes isn't enough. In the past hour, I have checked my e-mail three times. I sent a note to a friend about a magazine piece she's helping me with. I received a photo from my husband with a picture of a car he thought I might like. I have gone on Facebook once. I have received two texts.

Well, that's okay, you might be thinking to yourself. What's the harm in taking a couple of minutes to check in online? After all, isn't a quick glance at your e-mails, Twitter feed, the Facebook status updates of all your friends kind of like a twenty-first-century version of the cigarette break?

This may be the most important piece of advice I can give you: *The Internet is nothing like a cigarette break*. If anything, it's the opposite. One of the most difficult practical challenges facing writers in this age of connectivity is the fact that the very instrument on which most of us write is also a portal to the outside world. I once heard Ron Carlson say that composing on a computer was like writing in an amusement park. Stuck for a nanosecond? Why feel it? With the single click of a key we can remove ourselves and take a ride on a log flume instead.

By the time we return to our work—if, indeed, we return to our work at all—we will be further away from our deepest impulses rather than closer to them. Where were we? Oh, yes. We were stuck. We were feeling uncomfortable and lost. And how are we now? More stuck. More uncomfortable and lost. We have gained nothing in the way of waking-dream time. Our thoughts have not drifted but, rather, have ricocheted from one bright and shiny thing to another.

If the Internet had been in wide use during the time I quit smoking, I know what I would have been doing in that small borrowed room. I would have spent my days screwing around online. As it is—even after all the books and a lifetime of some pretty decent habits—I still find it enormously difficult to resist its lure. But on the best days, I imagine myself back to a place free of texts and tweets and Facebook messages. Free of the noise and Pavlovian thrill of an ever-filling in-box. I align myself with Donald Hall, rising with the dawn on his grandparents' farm; Virginia Woolf in her Bloomsbury writing room; Proust in his bed; Paul Auster making the morning trek to his monastic Brooklyn brownstone studio. And I am back in that room: the blank walls, the empty courtyard, the thin line of smoke spiraling out the window. The vast, wide-open world of the mind drifting, unmoored.

CHARACTER

Elderly people are not always craggy, wrinkled, stooped over, forgetful, or wise. Teenagers are not necessarily rebellious, querulous, or pimple-faced. Babies aren't always angelic, or even cute. Drunks don't always slur their words. Characters aren't *types*. When creating a character, it's essential to avoid the predictable. Just as in language we must beware of clichés. When it comes to character, we are looking for what is true, what is not always so, what makes a character unique, nuanced, indelible.

This specificity applies, obviously, to our main characters, but it is equally important when creating our minor characters: the man at the end of the bar, the receptionist in the doctor's office, the woman with the shopping bag on the street. They don't exist simply to advance our protagonist from point A to point B. They are not filler—you know, simply there to supply some local color. There is no such thing as filler or local color in life, nor can there be on the page.

Ask of yourself: How does this character walk? How does she smell? What is she wearing? What *underwear* is she wearing? What are the traces of her accent? Is she hungry? Thirsty? Horny? What's the last book she read? What did she have for dinner last night? Is she a good dancer? Does she do the crossword puzzle in pen? Did she have a childhood pet? Is she a dog person or a cat person?

Not that you would ever supply any—much less all—of these details. But you need to know them. A fairly popular writing class suggestion is to write a complete dossier of your character, complete with geneology, habits, physical traits, and so forth. I've never been a big fan of this exercise, because I do believe that the writing of lists and backstory can leach the process of its magic. However, if you live with a character for long enough—and deeply enough—in your imagination, you will know them the way you know a family member. Nothing can possibly stump you. Favorite food? Allergies? Secret shame? Annoying habit? Once formed, our characters occupy some part of our consciousness during our every waking and dreaming moment.

We—none of us—are ever clichés. We are the sum total of our stories. We may appear to be a type, a certain kind of person—a man, say, with a ruddy complexion, wearing a navy blue blazer with a silk pocket square, white trousers, no socks, suede loafers, a younger blonde woman on his arm. *Click, click, click,* your mind makes a snap judgment: rich businessman with a trophy wife. But what if this same man just got the news that he has prostate cancer? And that the young blonde on his arm is his daughter who has come to be with him during his upcoming surgery? That he was recently widowed? That he lost all his money to Bernie Madoff?

It is human nature to make these instant assumptions based on fleeting first impressions and our own biases and projections. But our job as writers is to look deeper. To hold in constant awareness just how much of the picture we may be missing. To train our empathetic imagination on all that we see.

DISTANCE

A friend who has had a long and successful career as a comedy writer tells me that people often ask him how he makes something funny. "I laugh first," he says. "Then I work backward from there. I don't think any lasting, timeless piece of art has ever begun with the writer sitting there thinking, 'oh, god, this is gonna slay them.'" Whether it's humor or pathos you're after on the page (and an argument could be made that the two are bedfellows), if you're feeling it while you're doing it, something's probably not right. In the movie *Something's Gotta Give,* Diane Keaton plays a successful playwright who laughs and cries and shakes her head ruefully as she sits in front of her computer, gaily writing, but in real life, a writer behaving this way might want to consider changing her meds. Grief, joy, hilarity, rage—all of it becomes the medium in which you work. You can't be feeling it and shaping it at the same time. On one of those scraps of paper I carry around in my Filofax, I keep the words of the playwright Edward Albee: "For the anger and rage to work aesthetically, the writer's got to distance himself from it and write in what Frank O'Hara referred to in one of his poems as 'the memory of my feelings.' Rage is incoherent. Observed rage can be coherent."

Another friend of mine, a gifted yoga teacher, ended a class once with a guided meditation that reminded me of Albee's words. As we sat on our mats with our eyes closed, Mitchel asked us to visualize a lit match or an incense stick, burning brightly. Then to imagine the flame going out. The tip burning red. Smoke rising, curling into the air. And finally, the cool ash. That image of the cool ash is one I've carried with me ever since, because it seems an apt metaphor for the creative process. We do not write out of the incoherent flame. Nor do we write out of the smoke. We wait until the ash is cool. It contains much of the matter within it that caused the flame, the smoke. Only now we can touch it. We can stick our finger into it. We can mold it at will. Now we can observe it. Now it is ours.

Edges

In his memoir, *Sic,* Joshua Cody—a musician, author, and cancer patient—writes that "the key to any composition, it occurs to me, is to write against an edge, a frame. Put a frame around something, anything—the frame of cancer, say, around a life, and you've already gotten somewhere, without even willing it."

But wait—what does this mean? Haven't I been pretty insistent about the idea that structure emerges from the writing itself? So what's up with this frame business? Am I contradicting myself? Well, not exactly! I'd like to respond. And, while I'm at it, I'm so pleased that you've been paying attention. But a frame isn't structure. Structure happens within the frame, but it isn't the frame. A frame keeps you in line. It lets you know when you've strayed from your story. A frame, writing against an *edge,* to use Cody's phrase, can be enormously help-ful in giving you clarity about your particular corner of the crazy-quilt. Your patch of land. Your precise and unique bit of geography. Your world.

For the sake of clarity, let's think of this in terms of modern memoir. In Tobias Wolff's *This Boy's Life,* a frame around the story is childhood, as it is in Frank McCourt's *Angela's Ashes,* or Frank Conroy's *Stop-Time.* In Susanna Kaysen's *Girl, Inter-rupted* or Martha Manning's *Undercurrents,* the frame is men-tal illness. In Caroline Knapp's *Drinking: A Love Story,* Pete Hamill's *A Drinking Life,* and David Carr's *The Night of the Gun,* the frame is addiction. In Lucy Grealy's *Autobiography of a Face* and Emily Rapp's *Poster Child,* it's disfigurement. In Pa-tricia Hampl's *Virgin Time* and Mary McCarthy's *Memories of a Catholic Girlhood,* the edges are defined by spiritual hunger. In Kathryn Harrison's *The Kiss,* it's incest. In Vivian Gornick's *Fierce Attachments,* it's the mother-daughter bond.

The frame offers parameters through which you can see your story. Without knowing what these parameters are, these edges, you will be in danger of throwing everything in there: the kitchen sink approach. Not everything belongs. It's not all equally compelling or resonant. This is true whether you're writing fiction or nonfiction. A frame creates, by necessity, dis-cernment. This, not that. The extraneous, the indulgent, the superfluous fall away. The frame "already gets you somewhere," to use Cody's words, "without even willing it." Which is not to say that addiction stories don't include childhood. Or that a story whose frame is the mother-daughter bond might not also be a spiritual quest. But if you know your frame, if you hew to it, it will create a kind of discipline around the telling of your story. It will require you to make creative decisions. Above all, it reminds you that this is a story you're telling. Here's a window. Look through it. What do you see? Sure, you're standing in a house that contains other windows. You can look through them another time. But stop here, for a while, at this window. There's so much to see.

Mondays

Monday mornings are often a challenge for me. Weekends are devoted to family and friends, to piled-up household chores. Marketing, sneaker shopping, pantry cleaning. Paperwork. School tuition. Insurance claims. The printer needs a new toner cartridge. The batteries in the TV remote have died. We've run out of garbage bags. A flurry of e-mails planning my mother-in-law's upcoming birthday. The deeper I immerse myself in the details—and they are mostly pleasurable details—of my domestic life, the greater the distance I must travel to get back to the place from which I work.

Monday mornings, the journey back to that place sometimes feels unending. Many writers have some sort of split screen inside of them. On one side, the work. On the other, everything else. Each renders the other not quite real. When working, the rest of life recedes. And when running errands, putting a child to bed, sorting through tax receipts, the world of the imagination slips out of view. We can't attend to both at once. But this doesn't mean that writers have to be conflicted creatures, always giving something up, neglecting our families, or our health, or the joys of everyday life, sacrificing ordinary happiness on the altar of art.

Think of this distance we travel between home and work, between family and art, between our everyday responsibilities and the life of the imagination as our own version of a rush-hour commute. We're not standing on a platform, boarding a train, shouldering our way through crowds on our way from home to office—a ritual that creates its own buffer zone between the two traversed worlds—but we are still making a journey. It's a solitary trek, and to a casual observer it might not seem like we're going anywhere at all. We might, for instance, be sitting in the same exact spot. We might be wearing the same clothes we slept in, or maybe we've actually showered and put on a semblance of normal attire. But no matter. We are commuting inward. And on Monday mornings—or after a long holiday, a summer vacation, any time we have been away from the page—we have to be even more vigilant about that commute. We are traveling to that place inside ourselves—so small as to be invisible—where we are free to roam and play. So let the electric company wait. Let the mail pile up. Turn off the phone's ringer. The voices around us grow quiet and still. We travel as surely as we're in our cars, listening to NPR, our mug of coffee in its trusty cup holder. We know that once we enter the place from which we write, it will expand to make room for us. It will be wider than the world.

FLOW

My son recently played his own composition on the piano and sang in front of a sizable audience. Afterward, I asked him how he felt as he was performing. I wondered if he had been nervous or self-conscious. I have never really grown accustomed to playing the piano in public. My fingers shake. My body grows rubbery with stage fright, even when I know a piece cold. It's a good thing that I spend most of my life alone in a room, rather than in any kind of performance setting, which I could never have survived.

"I forgot anyone was there," Jacob told me after his recital. "I was just inside the music." That's what I'd thought, watching him. He looked comfortable. Completely at ease. Un-self-conscious. This struck me as the best possible news. He hadn't just forgotten the audience. He had forgotten *himself*. He hadn't been wondering how his hair looked. He wasn't panicked about making a mistake. To forget oneself—to lose oneself in the music, in the moment—that kind of absorption seems to be at the heart of every creative endeavor. It can be the deepest pleasure, though it doesn't always feel like pleasure. Not exactly.

In Mihaly Csikszentmihalyi's *Flow,* a book about the psychology of optimal experience, the author describes these moments as occuring "when a person's body or mind is stretched to its limits in a voluntary effort to accomplish something difficult and worthwhile." But he goes on to warn us that this is not necessarily pleasant. We don't always get to feel unadulterated joy when we are in the midst of an optimal experience. Think of it as joy deferred. The work itself can be challenging to the point of physical and psychic pain. "I hate writing. I love having written," Dorothy Parker once said. The runner whose thighs burn with every step; the mathematician wrestling with a seemingly impossible equation; the chef tasting his béchamel sauce, focused on the precise balance of the milk and roux. And the writer? Well, one solitary writer in her Connecticut farmhouse is backed into a corner of her chaise longue, every muscle tense with effort. She is in the middle. The red hot center. This is what she's signed on for. She remembers that she is in the ocean with no land in sight, and she is building the boat. This demands all of her attention and holds it. Her coffee has long grown cold at her side. The dogs, sensing her struggle, have slunk out of the room. She is trying, oh, how she is trying, to get it right.

"The race is not to the swift, nor the battle to the strong . . .
but time and chance happen to them all."

—Ecclesiastes

The Best Part

If you show up, if you spend many hours alone, if you wage a daily battle with your inner censor, if you endure, if you put one word in front of the next until a long line of words is formed, a line that could stretch halfway across your home, if you take two steps forward, three steps back, if you grapple with bouts of despair and hopelessness—there will come a time when you can sense that the end is not too far away. This will carry its own quiet but unmistakable confidence. You will cast aside your doubt, your skepticism, your fear that perhaps you've been fooling yourself all along. You can no longer tell yourself it's never going to happen, because it *is* happening. Your breath deepens. Your field of vision widens.

Revel in it. Take your time.

This is the best part.

If beginnings are leaps of faith, and middles are vexing, absorbing, full of trap doors and wrong turns and dead ends, sensing an ending is your reward. It's better than selling your book. It's better than a good review. When you're in the home stretch, it seems the universe reaches out to support you. It meets you more than halfway. Whatever you still need in order to finish your novel, your story, your memoir, appears as if by the decree of some literary deity who understands just how hard you've worked, just how much you've struggled, and will now give you a break. A strain of music overheard on the street. A few sentences of dialogue. An interview on the car radio that solves a problem you didn't even know you had.

Sure-footedly, you move forward. It's not so much that you know where you're going. You may very well not. But the landscape you now inhabit has a quality of déjà vu. Somewhere in the recesses of your imagination, you've been here before. You recognize it as it builds. *Of course,* you think to yourself. *Exactly.* It isn't you, writing now. Not quite. This thing you have built in the dark, that has felt so many times like it might be your undoing, is now leading you along like a gentle giant. You don't know what the ending is—but you have a feeling about it. There's a tonal quality. Perhaps an image. There will be a moment—today, tomorrow, three weeks or two months from now—when you'll write a sentence and then stare at it, dumbfounded. It has caught you unawares. You can't be on the lookout for it. You can't will it, or force it, and you don't have to, because it will feel inevitable. Everything has led to this.

EXPOSURE

I can almost always feel the comment—more question than comment, really—in the second before it's spoken. The air stills and my nerves ready themselves, sensing imminent danger. *What's it like to reveal so much about yourself?* The person saying this searches my face for signs or clues—confirmation that this is, in fact, the case. There is the groping for words. A nod to the strangeness of the interaction. Perhaps even, in certain cases, the faintest whiff of distaste. Then, finally: *How do you do it? Don't you feel exposed?*

Over the years, I have learned to deflect this exchange so that it doesn't leave its trace on me. So that those words don't add up, stick to one another, form a residue. When faced with the exposure question, I bring to mind a conversation I once witnessed between the memoirist Frank McCourt and a woman he'd just met at a dinner party.

Her: *I feel like I know everything about you.*

Him (not even blinking): *Oh, darlin'. It's just a book.*

It's just a book. He delivered it with impeccable timing, and in the kindest possible way but it . . . well . . . it shut her up. But the truth is that we can feel exposed by our books—if we let that happen. And not just the memoirists among us. Fiction can be even more exposing than memoir—a map to the inner world, the subconscious internal workings, the obsessions and fears and secret joys of the writer. So as we're finishing, as we reach the end of a process that has been private and solitary, if we find ourselves starting to wonder what people will think of us, out there in the wide world, I would suggest that there's a very different way of considering this question of exposure.

You have not stripped naked.

This thing you've been writing is not a diary.

Quite the opposite.

Contrary to the notion that you've splattered your most intimate feelings all over the page, that you are now visible without even knowing it, as if standing spread-eagled in one of those airport security machines that can see through your clothes, you have, rather, chosen every single word. You've crafted each sentence. You've decided what to put in, what to leave out. You have chinked away, bit by bit, at a story. Creating something where before there was nothing. This story has taken and shaped your history, your heritage, your subconscious mind, your ideas, traumas, concerns. And if you've done your job it has also transformed all this raw data, this noisy chorus, into something cohesive and rewarding.

If literature is, to use Updike's phrase, that "most subtle instrument of self-examination known to man," it is also only thus because the writer has caught and wound herself around the thread of the universal. The truest and most artful self-revelation occurs when the self is subsumed to the art. The self becomes merely the vehicle. The art does not say *look at me*. If anything, it reflects ourselves back at us, saying: *look at yourself.*

And so. I cannot tell you that you will not be on the receiving end of the raised eyebrow, the small smile, the presumed intimacy with those who will think that now they know you. I cannot tell you that these moments will not bring with them an unease, a discomfort that will (irony alert!) in fact make you feel—however briefly—exposed by the very question. But I can tell you that the writing of a book, no matter how deeply, profoundly personal—if it is literature, if you have attended to the formidable task of illuminating the human heart in conflict with itself—will do the opposite of expose you. It will connect you. With others. With the world around you. With yourself.

RISK

The writer Valerie Martin once said that there are three kinds of dispositions: a good disposition, a bad disposition, and a writer's disposition. This simple statement has stayed with me because there is something about the writer's disposition—or the artistic temperament—that requires a particular fusing of traits. If any one of these traits is missing, the whole delicate apparatus will eventually fall apart.

There is the gift, of course, which is inseparable from—though not the same as—a need, a hunger for expression. It is possible to have the gift without the need. It is also possible to have the need without the gift. The former can lead to a happy and contented life. I have seen promising young writers discard their gift, shrugging it off like a wrap on a warm summer evening. They don't care. They don't want or need it. The other, however, is a painful situation: the hunger for self-expression without the gift—that ineffable thing you can't teach, or buy, or will into being. This story often ends in resentment and unfulfillment. Then there is endurability—Ted Solotaroff's word—the ability to withstand the years in the cold, the solitary life, the affronts and indignities, the painful rejections that never end. The gift and the hunger are nothing without that endurability. But up there with the gift, the hunger, and endurance is another trait, without which the writer's life can't possibly work.

Remember that *New Yorker* cartoon about writer's block? In the frame entitled "Writer's Block: Permanent," the writer is standing in front of a fish store bearing his name. While this cartoon is about that old bugaboo, writer's block, it's also about risk aversion. The writer-turned-fishmonger caved in to what John Gregory Dunne called "failure of nerve." And even though he's just a cartoon character, I think of him often. His resigned posture. His joyless gaze into the middle distance.

The writing life is full of risk. There is the creative risk—the willingness to fall flat on our face again and again—but there is also practical risk. As in, *it may not work out.* We don't get brownie points for trying really hard. When we set our hopes on this life, we are staking our future on the contents of our own minds. On our ability to create and continue to create. We have nothing but this. No 401(k), no pension plan, often no IRA, no plans—god knows—for retirement. We have to accept living with profound uncertainty. I have a friend, a talented journalist with a solid but undecorated career, who has made his choices, again and again, based on his assessment of safety. This assignment and not that one. This book proposal. That magazine contract. When I listen to him talk about his fears—what will happen when he gets older, when he and his wife can't work as hard anymore, when it's time for their kids to go to college—he unwittingly throws me into a panic. I become acutely aware of the choices that I have made, and continue to make every day—well into midlife now.

There are no half measures when it comes to risk. Risk means that gut-wrenching feeling, having your heart in your throat, not knowing what the next book is, not knowing where the next check is coming from or when, not being able to project a year, two, or ten into the future, not having a plan. Which is not to say that writers are irresponsible children. I have a mortgage that somehow gets paid each month, along with health insurance premiums. My husband and I have modest savings and wills. But our finances would give my journalist friend a heart attack. We are always one potential disaster away from . . . well, potential disaster. A health crisis. A tree falling on the roof. A disability. What then?

Of course this keeps me up at night. My husband and I walk a path lit by uncertainty. We are always accommodating to a new situation. We never know what the next day will bring. Our lives are affected by other people's opinions and decisions. We are building skyscrapers from the top down. Sometimes, we end up with a pile of rubble. Occasionally, a gleaming tower.

Our son has a front-row seat to our joys and disappointments. One year, in Paris, the three of us went out to a late dinner to celebrate my memoir *Devotion*'s improbable and completely unexpected appearance near the top of the *Los Angeles Times* best-seller list. Another year, he saw his father, pale and anxious because an investor had pulled out of a film that had already gone into preproduction.

But what I hope is that Jacob sees his parents doing what they love, doing what they *must*. Every day is different. Surprises happen. In our household, it's feast or famine. All this may make him want to be a fishmonger when he grows up. He may long for security and consistency. And who could blame him? But if he is an artist—if he possesses that fusion of gift, hunger, endurability, and, finally, a willingness to embrace risk—he won't have much choice in the matter. This life chooses us.

On Having the Last Word

I can't tell you when my mother and I began the fight that lasted the whole of our lives together but I know the moment it ended. On a beautiful late spring evening, I pulled into my driveway and saw Michael standing on our front porch, phone in hand. I lowered my car window and he looked at me and I knew that my mother was dead.

The final years of our relationship had been marked by long periods of estrangement. When Jacob was ill, I couldn't tolerate her selfishness, her sudden rages. Even this—my child's illness—became a weapon in her hands, one that she used to hurt me. The more I pulled away in order to protect myself, the more she went on the attack. I stopped answering phone calls, letters, faxes, messages, UPS deliveries. Everything I had in me—everything I had to give—went to my son. It was only after Jacob was stable and my mother was diagnosed with terminal lung cancer that I once again tried to be a daughter to her. I visited her in the city, held her hand at doctors' appointments, brought her to our home in Connecticut. As she drifted in and out of consciousness, I sat by her bedside. Friends suggested that this was an opportunity for closure; perhaps she and I would finally be able to talk things through. But I don't believe in closure. My relationship with my mother was going to die as it had lived: tortured, dangling, forever mired in lost opportunity and sorrow.

The most difficult writing assignment I have ever undertaken was my mother's eulogy. There were no other children. No friends. Hardly any family. I wanted to be true to my mother—to her vitality, her powerful instinct for survival—but I also wanted to be true to myself. As I wrestled with what to say, I came to realize something profound: because I was alive, and she was dead, I would, for the rest of my life, have the last word.

Up until the time that she fell ill, my mother had a voice—and she used it. If she felt angered, or wronged, by something I had written, she wrote to me, or called and yelled; she wrote to newspapers; she complained to booksellers; she proposed that the 92nd Street Y allow her to teach a course about the mother and daughter in Jewish literature. During the years of our estrangement, she showed up at my readings and glared at me from the back row. When it came to my writing life, her rage was part of our dialogue. I wrote, she ranted. But then she was dead. Gone. She would never again fight back. I could write whatever I wanted, with no fear of wounding her, and without fear of repercussion.

Right?

Well, no. Not quite. Because I have discovered that having the last word comes with some very heavy baggage. After a person is gone, everything we write about them becomes a eulogy of sorts. It extends and expands their identity and reputation in the world, even if just among a group of readers. Literature is more permanent than the characters who live within its pages. And so the grappling begins. We weigh our responsibilities against our creative impulses. We wonder if simply being aware is enough—its own protection against doing damage. We decide, ultimately, what we, the living, can live with. Because we do have the last word—all of us, whether writers or not. Because we are here, walking this earth, striding over bones, breathing ashes. We remember. That memory is part of our consciousness. And if we are writers, we do what writers do with our consciousness: we set pen to page and see what emerges. We do not do so with impunity but, rather, with grave misgivings, courage, empathy, discomfort. With unresolveable questions in our hearts. We know that some day we, too, will be gone. That this last word is fleeting. That this last word is not, in fact, the last word. But it is all we have.

TRIBE

As I write these words, I am, of course, alone. It's the middle of the day and I have barely stepped outside except to pick up a couple of envelopes full of books and manuscripts that FedEx left on the porch. I have spoken to no one since seven o'clock this morning. I'm wearing the ratty T-shirt I slept in last night. The house is silent. A crow caws outside my office window.

These solitary days are my lifeline. They are the lifeline of every writer I know. We hold on to our solitude, fiercely protect these empty days. But at the same time, we long for community. We have no water cooler. No office gossip. No Friday night drinks after work. No weekend softball game. We're outcasts and loners, more comfortable being out of step than part of a group. If pressed, you'd find that most of us had not pledged sororities or fraternities in college. We don't tend to be members of clubs. We approach themed parties, baby showers, boys' nights out, with something like dread. Back when I lived in Brooklyn, our house was in a neighborhood lousy with writers. A quick trip to the corner bodega meant running into writer friends who were out buying a roll of paper towels, sneaking a cigarette. And though from my rural hill, it's easy to feel sentimental about those encounters, at the time, I recall a certain discomfort on both sides, especially if it was in the midst of a writing day. We liked each other, sure—we might even have a plan to meet later that evening for a drink—but right then we didn't necessarily want to be reminded of each other's existence. We were *working*.

This prickly, overly sensitive, socially awkward group of people is my tribe. If you're a writer, they're yours as well. This is why I've never really understood competition and envy among writers. We are competing with ourselves—not with each other. And when we do encounter each other, whether at readings, or conferences, or online, hopefully we recognize ourselves and the strange existence we all share. We realize that we are part of the same species and that we need one another to survive. Though we write our books alone, ultimately everything we do involves some collaboration. Every good book you'll ever read has the thumbprints of other writers all over it. As we finish a manuscript we may find ourselves thinking of who to turn to, who can help us. Who will read us with generosity and intelligence and care. From where I sit, I can see a pile of manuscripts and galleys across my office floor. They are books by students, former students, teaching colleagues, friends, and strangers—sent to me for blurbs, or with requests to help them find an agent, or whatever. I try to help when I can. When the work is good, I'm eager to be a part of ushering it into the world. Nothing excites me more than wonderful writing. It lifts me up. It shows me what is possible. And it makes me feel connected to this larger community of writers in the world.

A long time ago, I sent a draft—actual manuscript pages— of an early novel to an idol of mine, the writer Tim O'Brien whose *The Things They Carried* is one of my favorite books. I got his address from a friend, wrote him a note, and stuffed my manuscript into a manila envelope. I knew that many writers of his stature had sworn off blurbing, believing the whole process to be corrupted and ennervating (a view I sometimes share). I had, in fact, recently received a five-page, single-spaced, typewritten letter from a well-known American novelist, explaining to me his policy of not blurbing. Tim O'Brien and I shared no one in common. He was not a cousin of my best friend's best friend from camp. So I sent off my manuscript with no real hope. A couple of weeks later, I received a thin letter back. I stood in the lobby of my apartment building and ripped open the envelope.

Dear Dani Shapiro, it began. *It is now three o'clock in the morning—*

I began to cry.

—and I have just finished your beautiful book.

I can still see the black ink on the plain white sheet of typing paper, the handwritten scrawl. *I'm happy to offer a comment—*

Tim O'Brien had stayed up until three in the morning reading my manuscript. He opened the envelope, began to read, kept reading. He had then felt moved to write me back, along with precious words of support. These twenty years later, I still have not met Tim O'Brien but he is part of my community. I will forever be grateful to him, not only because of his act of generosity to a young writer, but also because he taught me a lesson I have come to live by. I don't forget what it was like. I reach out a hand when I can. I remind myself every day that it's about the work. I am here in Connecticut. You might be in Missoula, Montana, or Taos, New Mexico, or Portland, Oregon. You're in a café, or at a writers' conference, or at your kitchen table. The words have come easily to you today, or you feel like your head is about to explode. You're a household name, or laboring in obscurity. I am here, and you are there, and we are in this thing together.

Patience

I think of her still. She was one of my most gifted students, and she was endearing, vulnerable—the kind of young woman who compels you to take her under your wing. Which I did. I took her in, crossed all sorts of boundaries. I read and edited her work outside the confines of class, met her for coffee, for drinks, had her to my home for Thanksgiving. She was a quivering creature—everything about her shook: her hands, her legs, her voice. Her fingers—what I most remember are her fingers—bloody and raw, bitten to the quick. Her prose was a wild, galloping horse. Untamed and gorgeous. She ricocheted from the sacred to the ordinary and back again, jammed erudite references into brief asides, created worlds within worlds within worlds.

When she asked me—halfway through her first novel— what I thought about her getting an agent, I told her to wait. I urged her to finish it first. To spend more time writing in the dark. I counseled patience. She nodded, shook. Bit the skin around her fingernails. She was in a graduate writing workshop filled with good writers. They were all driven, all anxious about being young but not *that* young. How many years did they have before they would no longer be considered precocious? How many years to make the lists—you know, "Thirty-five under Thirty-five," "Twenty under Forty."

When she came back to class after winter break and told me that she had an agent, I wasn't surprised. And when the agent sold her unfinished first novel as well as an unwritten second novel in a two-book deal so substantial that it was covered in *New York Magazine,* I was also unsurprised. She was rare, an original. But I still felt she should have held off. The book wasn't ready, and now she had a deadline. She had an editor, a publisher, the pressure of a hefty book advance.

In my workshop full of panicked MFA students, I probably don't have to tell you how this news was greeted. Students wept in my office. They were sure this spelled the end for them—as if writing were a race. As if the success of one young writer somehow robs another. They were sure that she had grabbed the brass ring. That there *was* a brass ring. The delicate balance between creativity and ambition, patience and impatience, private and public had been upended.

I loved this young woman—her old soul, her stubborn streak, her huge heart—and so I wish I could tell you that her story turned out well. That, as her classmates believed, her early book deal presaged a lifetime of literary achievement and even personal contentment. Instead, she pushed to finish the novel, and it was published to little fanfare. Reviews were mixed. Critics were respectful of her talent but found the novel to be frustrating, undisciplined, uneven. Within a couple of years, it was out of print. She disappeared, ostensibly hard at work on her second novel. I lost touch with her but kept my eye out for her new book. It never came.

She taught, here and there. To my knowledge, she never published anything ever again. Not a story, not an essay, not a book review. Once, I ran into her in a Brooklyn restaurant and she was still that same, trembling creature, but now she had a brittleness to her, a distractibility that hadn't been there before. A number of years later, I received an e-mail with her name in the subject line and I knew she was dead. She had died of a heart attack in an East Village bodega at the age of forty.

Look, it's easy to sit here—my eyes brimming at the memory of her, at the loss of her—and speculate how it might have been different. If you change one thing in a narrative, everything else changes, too. What would have happened if she had waited, if she had taken the time to shape the book, to deepen it, to allow it to become its best possible self? If she had spent longer, writing in the dark?

A number of her classmates went on to have writing lives. They are novelists, short story writers, editors, professors. For some, it took five, ten, twelve years after graduation for their careers to take hold. A story here, a story there. Drawers full of rejection slips. Novels abandoned, buried in closets. Plenty of days, no doubt, filled with hopelessness, regret. Those writers who once wept in my office now know what it takes to build a creative life. To wake up each day and start anew. To shrug off humiliation, rejection, uncertainty. To avoid the impulse—like reaching for a drug—to skip steps, succumb impatiently, send out work before its ready. They have learned that there is no brass ring. That we can never know how it's going to turn out. That the race is not to the swiftest. I wonder if they think of her.

WHAT IS YOURS

I am a Jewish girl from New Jersey. Have I ever wished I came from somewhere else? That the soil that grew me wasn't New Jersey—which, while the birthplace of Philip Roth, is not a state known for its great literary landscape the way, say, Mississippi is (Faulkner! Welty!) or New England (Bishop! Dickinson! Thoreau!) or Nebraska (Cather!). But "geography is destiny," said Heraclitus. So is childhood. The atmosphere I breathed in as a child remains with me still. It is the basis of my material—my clay, my marble, my palette. It's what I've got.

Only child, older parents, their contentious marriage, observant Jew, religiously conflicted, suburban upbringing, child model, rebellious teen, tragic accident—are, on their own, just a list, but when woven together, begin to form nubs and knots, the texture of a fabric. Every writer has a fabric. The most intense moments of our lives seem to sharpen and raise themselves as if written in Braille—this is where our themes begin to take hold. Explore deeply enough and you will find strange and startling questions to grapple with on the page.

We do not choose this fabric as if browsing the aisles at Bloomingdale's. We don't get to say, *Hey, I really prefer that writer's life circumstances. I think I'll take the Southern Gothic childhood, the crazy alcoholic mother, the gunshot in the barn.* It doesn't work that way. Whether or not we are fond of our tiny corner of the universe, its all we've got. If we try to control it, if our egos get in the way and we decide that we want to be, say, a lyric poet, or a political satirist, or a writer of best-selling mysteries, or whatever it is that we think would be cool or important or fun, well, that is the surest way to a dead end and heartache. It is the truest lesson I know about writing—and about life—that we must always move in the direction of our own true calling, not anyone else's.

And so, when I am quietly at work, I can just about see my mother in an enormous, floppy hat and gardening gloves, beads of perspiration on the back of her neck, her freckled arms. I can catch a whiff of the oil refineries along the Jersey

Turnpike. As if from a great distance, I hear the garage door opening, signaling my father's return from his job in the city. *Wahoo,* he would call to my mother. His briefcase on the floor. His loosened tie. *Wahoo, I'm home!* The *whoosh, whoosh* of the pool-cleaning machine that circled the turquoise blue like a snake. The quiet Sabbath lunches, our three forks scraping against plates. The sadness I couldn't grasp, the suppressed rage. His bottles of pills. Her closets stuffed with designer clothing. The solo trips. The separate beds. My beautiful parents, their unrealized, unarticulated dreams slowly slipping from their grasp. Their love for one another, hopeless. The air thick with what was unsaid.

The unsaid.

I am spending my life trying to say it.

That is what is mine.

ECHO

When we are coming to the end of a piece of work, we may become aware of a desire to tie up all the loose ends. To wrap up the package in a pretty bow, every character, every situation resolved neatly. We have spent hundreds of hours inside the dilemmas, the internal lives of these characters, and very often we have fallen in love with them. We want to know, and we want the reader to know, that everything's going to turn out all right. Like the ends of those made-for-television movies that flash into the future, allowing us to see the fates of all the characters, we may be tempted to force resolution.

But think about life for a moment. If, in creating a world on the page, we are attempting to hold a mirror up to humanity, to illuminate something about our lives as we live them, how often do our stories end neatly and to our satisfaction? No. We are left with loose ends. We don't know what will happen next. We try to make sense of what has already happened, to understand the inherent messiness. To move forward in the darkness. That is part of our job, and it is most definitely the job of literature.

When I consider endings, I think of music—in particular, the experience of sitting in a concert hall at the end of a performance. If the music has hit its mark, a singular connection has been made and is being broken. But this break doesn't happen all at once. When those last notes have sounded, they linger. The music doesn't screech to a halt. It *can't*. We—the listener, the reader—have to lean into it. To meet it as it hangs in the air, as it fades away, until finally it is only memory.

All that sound! An orchestra filled with musicians making music—violins, violas, cellos, flutes, bassoons, French horns,

drums, cymbals—is alive. So much has gone on! So much invested, felt, experienced. The final notes are played—the last
page is turned—and then there is the echo. It vibrates through
the concert hall. The audience, the reader, waits—and in waiting, participates. In that echo is contained the chaos, regret,
untold joy, loss, randomness, possibility. In that echo there
exists the shape of the future, and the impossibility of our
knowing it. That echo is the longing—there is nothing more
human than this—for all that comes after.

BREAK

In the years we've spent writing, children may have been born.
Loved ones may have died. Perhaps we've moved from one
home to another. Or been rocked by a health crisis, a betrayal,
a divorce. And of course, there are the smaller fleas of life.
But somehow we've kept at it. We've followed our headlights
through the fog. We've muddled through on days when the
air around us has quivered like jello. We've shown up, even
when showing up was the last thing on earth we wanted to
do. And now, as we seem to be approaching something that
looks suspiciously like the end, we wonder what we have on
our hands. What is this unwieldy thing? Will it hold together?

Will it make sense—to ourselves, much less to anyone else? *What have we done?*

We may slow to a crawl at this point, not because we're savoring the moment, but because we're experiencing flashes of abject terror, a terror that disguises itself as the truth. We become convinced that we've spent years of our life on something that makes no sense, or not enough sense. Something that will never find its way into the world, or worse, will be roundly ridiculed, or worse, ignored. Who were we to think we could make this creative leap? What lunacy made us think we could take these images, thoughts, sounds, phrases, memories, and ideas floating before us like dust motes, and craft them into a story that might speak to others?

But there's good news: the door isn't locked. You can escape. If you find yourself wanting to step away—if you're hunched over your notebook or your screen with every muscle in your body tense from the secret certainty that you've wasted months (years!) on this impossible thing before you—then step away. If you're nearing the end, you're in no danger of losing whatever it is you already have on the page. The momentum of all that work—those days when you stayed in the chair—will be there to support you. If beginnings require fortitude, and middles stamina—if, to paraphrase Annie Dillard, your work is a lion in a cage in your study, a wild thing you must visit every day in order to reassert your mastery over it—endings ask of you only that you take a step back. A day off? Two? Three? A long walk? A drive in the country? A bath? A few stiff drinks with a friend? All of the above? Go for it, I say. Take a break if you need one. Turn down that noisy mind and come back to the page later. That wild animal has taken a nap and is sitting contentedly in a corner of your study, chewing on the rug. You will finish. You have fashioned a world. It's terrifying and exhilarating. If you have a pulse, this is exactly how you should feel. What have you done? You don't know yet. When you're ready, sit down again anew. You'll find out.

DANCE

When we moved from the city to the country, I discovered that our small town (population 3124) was the improbable home to two well-known dance companies. These troupes had a complicated history with each other: scorned lovers, defectors, enemies, grudging admirers. You could spot the dancers across the café, or in the aisles of the local market, or gassing up their cars. They were lean, of course, and sinewy, with veined arms, rounded biceps, clavicles that could cut through ice. But it wasn't just the sheer, crazy beauty of them among the often soft and paunchy New Englanders as it was the *grace* of them.

When I was invited to sit in on rehearsals I became fascinated not only by their process, but by my response to it. I related intensely to what I was seeing in the rehearsal hall, even though it technically had nothing to do with the way I spent my own days. I was often inert, almost always alone. Sometimes, during a long writing day, I'd catch a glimpse of myself, a reflection in a mirror or a window, and be startled that I even had a physical form. These dancers were in constant motion, electrifyingly, necessarily corporeal and present. Still, I felt a kinship with them. The essence of our work—whether the forming of a shape or a sentence, a dance or a novel—comes from the same willingness to fall, to fail. To surrender.

All through that long, hot summer, I spent hours each day watching dances being made. One of the artistic directors was reading Emily Dickinson. Why? Were there the beginnings of a dance—a gesture—to be found in the poet's distilled words, as old and deep as geodes? I asked him, and, shrugging, he told me he didn't yet know. I didn't know, either, what I was doing there as I listened to the soft thuds bare feet made as they hit the hard wood floor. The heavy wind of bodies pulled through space. The rise and fall of rib cages, panting from the exertion. Limbs glistening with sweat. These bodies and their relationship to one another became, for a while, my poetry.

To allow ourselves to spend afternoons watching dancers rehearse, or sit on a stone wall and watch the sunset, or spend the whole weekend rereading Chekhov stories—to know that we are doing what we're supposed to be doing—is the deepest form of permission in our creative lives. The British author and psychologist Adam Phillips has noted, "When we are inspired, rather like when we are in love, we can feel both unintelligible to ourselves and most truly ourselves." This is the feeling I think we all yearn for, a kind of hyperreal dream state. We read Emily Dickinson. We watch the dancers. We research a little known piece of history obsessively. We fall in love. We don't know why, and yet these moments form the source from which all our words will spring.

BETRAYAL

The poet was being interviewed onstage. She had recently published a memoir about her father, an eminent bishop. She was the bishop's daughter, which was also the title of her memoir. Her father had been bisexual. The secrecy surrounding this fact had thrown a heavy cloak over her childhood and early adulthood, and much of her inner world—depression, anxiety, alcoholism, not to mention her own sexuality—had been tangled up in it. For the better part of five years she worked on this book—probing her memory while at the same time reporting and researching. Along the way she discovered—and met with—the man who had been her father's great love. The memoir was a tour de force of writing and of *living*—a valiant and painstaking excavation of a particular truth: her own. Of course she had a right to tell her own truth. Didn't she?

As I sat in the audience, I felt anxious for the poet, Honor Moore, who was my friend. She had been visibly trembling as I drove her to the event. Her memoir had caused an uproar in her family. She had committed an unpardonable sin, it seemed. She had broken ranks to tell the story that had been kept secret for decades. Several of her siblings had written letters to *The New Yorker,* where an excerpt had run, expressing their outrage. These letters were followed by an avalanche of toxic online comments. A gentle poet, a teacher of writing, she was now a lightning rod for controversy. Some were saying she should have known this would happen. Others, that the book was a calculated bid for the kind of publicity a poet would not normally receive. Either way, she was this moment's poster child for literary betrayal.

Onstage her interviewer ran through questions about voice and narrative, poetry and memoir, and then brought up the letters to *The New Yorker.*

"Can we talk about your family's response to the book?"

Honor was wearing an ankle-length black skirt and a flowing blouse, with flat shoes that seemed to anchor her to the ground. Her gray-black hair shone in the spotlight. She was not a young woman. She had been through plenty.

"I believe that we don't choose our stories," she began, leaning forward. "Our stories choose us." She paused and took a sip of water. Her hand, I noticed, was steady. "And if we don't tell them, then we are somehow diminished."

Diminished. The word went through me like a bolt. I pulled out the small notebook I carry with me and scribbled down what she had just found the grace to say.

There it was. All of it. I thought of my favorite passage in the Gnostic Gospels: *If we bring forth what is within us, it will save us. If we do not bring forth what is within us, it will destroy us.* And what the Bhagavad Gita has to say about dharma: *Better is one's own dharma though imperfectly carried out than the dharma of another carried out perfectly.*

I knew about the struggle for authenticity. The mining for words to collect together what felt impossibly broken. I wanted to gather up in my arms all that was lost to me. I wanted nothing less than to remake my world. A writer afraid of her own subject—whatever it might be—is a frozen creature, trapped in the inessential. *Diminished.*

"It steadies me to tell these things," wrote Seamus Heaney in his poem "Crossings." Honor had written a story that was essential to her. She had faced herself on the page: her demons, her fears, her own fallibility. In order to tell her story she'd included others—mother, father, siblings, lovers—because she hadn't lived in a vacuum. She was her own narrative's central character, but there were other necessary supporting ones. My mother's voice came flooding back to me. *What right? How dare you?* An aunt's coldness that never thawed after my first memoir was published. An uncle's only comment a request that I insert errata into future editions to correct a misspelling of his wife's name. A half-sister, on a meditation retreat in Poland (on the train tracks of Auschwitz), who reportedly overheard a group of people discuss my second memoir—a book in which she does not appear—and interrupted them to announce: *I'm the evil half-sister.*

Janet Malcolm has called journalism morally indefensible. "The business of art is theft, is armed robbery, is not pleasing your mother." Joan Didion referred to writing as the tactic of a secret bully. We will do what we must. Our lives are our material. (My mother once asked me if I really needed to include, in an essay published in *The New York Times,* the details of the first nonkosher meal she ever ordered in front of me—a bacon cheeseburger. Oh, yes. Yes, I did.)

Will I ever be entirely comfortable with the ruthlessness of revelation? Will you? Mostly likely not. It's an uncomfortable existence we've chosen—or perhaps that has chosen us. But still, I do not believe that we are monsters. We search for the line between what is essential—and possibly hurtful—and what is superfluous—and possibly hurtful. We become aware of our own power and try to use it wisely. There is no room for clever pot shots. For making ourselves look good at another's expense. For using our pen for revenge. The stakes are high. The stakes are love and—yes—honor, and moral responsibility. We ask ourselves *why*—Why this story? Why this moment? Is it necessary? If we are vigilant, we will know when we are betraying others and when we are in danger of diminishing ourselves.

LOST FINGERS

When the great jazz guitarist Django Reinhardt was eighteen, his left hand was badly burned in a fire and he lost the use of his third and fourth fingers. He was told he'd never play the guitar again—but instead, he used his two good fingers for solos, his injured ones for chord work, and created his own musical style. He compensated for his weakness—he worked with it, he understood it—and in so doing, developed something stronger and richer because of it.

We all have our lost fingers. Just as what was unavailable to Django Reinhardt informed the way he played music, what is absent—or out of reach—will inform our voice. In part, we write from the tension of what we cannot do. That tension pushes us into dark corners where, Houdini-like, we have to perform feats seemingly beyond our capabilities to wriggle our way out.

My husband's latest film project was originally set on a long, sandy stretch of a Florida key where modern high-rises had sprung up like cliffs along the dunes. As he thought about directing this film—as he cast it, secured financing, hired crew—in his mind, the story was always going to unfold against this backdrop of Florida's west coast, its ocean a precise deep blue, its sunsets fiery orange, reflected against the sliding glass doors and balconies of the condominiums that line the beach. But as the budgetary constraints of filmmaking settled in, it became clear that the film might need to be shot elsewhere—in another state, with no high-rises lining the beach, and different light, and different sunsets. I watched as he struggled with this change of plan. He called me from a location-scouting trip to North Carolina, his voice sounding drained. "We may have to shoot in a house instead of a condo," he said. "I don't know. It's not what I pictured."

I thought of Django Reinhardt's lost fingers. I thought of a friend's daughter, a dwarf who had become a competitive rider, tall and graceful in her saddle. And I thought of the way I feel—as I near the end of every book I write—constrained by the narrative structure I've chosen. We are always coming face-to-face with our limits, or with the limits that the world imposes upon us.

If we are artists—hell, whether or not we're artists—it is our job, our responsibility, perhaps even our sacred calling, to take whatever life has handed us and make something new, something that wouldn't have existed if not for the fire, the genetic mutation, the sick baby, the accident. To hurl ourselves in an act of faith so complete that our fears, insecurities, hopelessness, and despair blur along the edges of our vision. We stop for nothing. It doesn't matter that no one has ever done it before—become a blues guitarist with two working fingers, been a dwarf in a show-jumping competition, turned North Carolina into Florida. It is in the leap that the future unfolds, surprising us with what can be done.

STEWARD

I need to live by certain rules in order to protect my writing life. When I was starting out, I didn't understand this. An old friend would call and ask me to lunch, or worse, breakfast, and I'd jump at the chance to get up from my desk for a couple of hours and join the world of real people eating real meals. I convinced myself that I had enough discipline to go out for a bit and then return to my desk, perhaps even invigorated and refreshed. And so I would head out, full of high hopes—a quick lunch, then back to work!—and then, an hour or two later, I would discover that my day was over. I had ruined it with conversation, laughter, waiters offering fizzy water or flat. I had stomped all over it by being out and about like someone with an actual lunch break. Overstimulated, squinting in the sunlight like a displaced nocturnal creature, I'd wander the streets of New York in a stupor. I'd find myself in the dressing room of a boutique, trying on a silk blouse. I'd call another friend and meet for tea. I was out already, after all. Why not just make a day of it, and stay out for dinner? Go see a play in my new silk blouse? Get a nightcap? I'm reminded of a wonderful essay by Amy Hempel on why she chose not to have children, in which she imagines, at one moment, putting her baby down for a nap, then deciding to go out to buy diapers, then taking in a movie, then flying to Paris, having forgotten all about her sleeping baby.

Holidays were also a problem. Every year, the Fourth of July, or Memorial Day weekend, or Martin Luther King Jr. Day would roll around, and I would feel that I should do whatever it was that the rest of the world was doing. But our work doesn't know it's a holiday. Our work requires us to adhere to certain rules—not because we're rigid or self-absorbed as frustrated friends or family might secretly think—but because it's the only way we can do it. If we are deep inside a story, we're in another world—the world we've created—which, for the time being, is where we need to live if we are to make it real to ourselves and, ultimately, to others.

I used to be angry with myself for my inability to live a normal life with normal rhythms, and also be a writer. But I've come to believe that *normal* is overrated—for artists, for everyone. When I was writing *Devotion,* all but the most essential tasks fell away. My hair got too long; I skipped my annual mammogram; the dogs' nails went unclipped; the windows didn't get cleaned; I lost touch with friends. But I took care of my family, and my book got written. That was all I could manage.

As you near the end, you will likely feel selfish. You will want to do everything you can to protect your instrument— which is to say, yourself—as you inch toward the finish line. This is as it should be, as it *must* be, if your work is to reach its potential. Embrace this selfishness, for now. Wrap it around you like a quilt made of air. Let no one inside of it except those you love the most. Don't leave that essential place. *Be a good steward to your gifts.* This is the first sentence on a list I keep tacked to the bulletin board in my study, an impeccable set of instructions left by the poet Jane Kenyon.

Protect your time.
Feed your inner life.

Avoid too much noise.
Read good books, have good sentences in your ears.
Be by yourself as often as you can.
Walk.
Take the phone off the hook.
Work regular hours.

No to lunch with friends, to the overflowing in-box. Quiet contemplation will lead you to riches, so keep good literature on your bedside table and read for a few minutes before you go to sleep instead of, say, passing out during episode five of season three of *Mad Men*. Cultivate solitude in your writing space, in the car, at the kitchen table when the house is empty. Get your blood moving. Feel your feet on the earth. Your mind is not floating in space but connected to a body. Kenyon wrote this before the lure of the Internet became like crack cocaine for most writers, so I would add "Disable the Internet." Find a rhythm. This is wisdom from a poet who died too young. I never knew her but she has helped me as much as anyone I have ever known.

WORKSHOP

For twenty years, I have taught writing workshops—under flickering fluorescent lights in a YMCA basement that smelled of chlorine; in a dusty Colorado mining town; in urban university classrooms; on the leafy quads of New England colleges; on a retrofitted crabbing vessel moored on an Alaskan island; in a former monastary in the Berkshire mountains; in a beach cottage in Provincetown; in a sunny antique-filled room high above the Amalfi Coast, where coffee is brought out on silver trays; in my own living room. And still I am nervous before a first workshop.

I can spot the students, the ones who have come with their fragile egos, the voices in their heads shouting at them that they're no good, they're phonies, they're in the wrong place. Whether they've enrolled in a graduate writing program or signed up for a three-day retreat or flown halfway across the world to attend a conference—they're vulnerable. Some will hardly make eye contact, they're so shy. Others will posture, full of bluster, about stories they've published, or nearly published, or contests they've won. They will find their seats—around the table, or on sofas. They will fiddle with the tops of their pens. Dig through their bags for chewing gum. Take one last look at their cell phones.

At the moment when we finally begin—when I look around the room—they have no idea that I haven't been able to eat breakfast (or lunch, or dinner). That I have just gone into the ladies room to have a little talk with myself, in which I remind myself that I'm good at what I do—that it pretty much always turns out well. What they see is a woman—a writer they've chosen to study with—in front of them, looking calm and comfortable. She's done this hundreds of times before, hasn't she? She's published how many books? She takes her place, draws her legs beneath her, leans forward. Puts on her glasses. Clears her throat. *Hi, everyone.*

A workshop that goes wrong can derail a writer. A teacher who abuses her power and responsibility—either directly or indirectly—can have a lasting negative impact. Laziness, egomania, ineptitude—over the years I've cleaned up plenty of other teachers' messes. And so during these opening hours, my aim is to cast a protective net over the whole lot of them. We—this ragtag group of ten or twelve—are going to become a single organism. A collective unconscious. We are going to set aside our petty concerns and focus, instead, on the sentences in front of us. We will train our *best selves*—our empathic understanding, our optimism, our critical eye—to understand what each of us is trying to do. We are going to laugh, possibly cry, argue, roll our eyes. But we're going to do it with respect, and even with love.

This love is a strange alchemy of mutual recognition. We are, each one of us, wrestling with words, with our futile stabs at some kind of human eloquence. We are solitary by nature but we have chosen to come together because the page benefits from the eyes of others. Because we are unable to see our own work clearly. Because we have developed connections and metaphors that are unknowable to us until someone else switches the lights on. We come to the workshop table—even the most defensive and cynical among us—in an act of faith. *See me*, we are saying. *See beneath my words to the truer words that rush in a river beneath. Plunge your hands into this river. Show me what I have done.*

ASTONISHMENT

The page—if you spend your life in deep engagement with it—will force you to surrender your skepticism. It will keep you open and undefended. It doesn't promise comfort. But if you hurl yourself at it, give it everything you've got, if you wake up each morning—bruised, bloody, aching—ready to throw yourself at it again, I'll make you a promise: it will keep you alive to what you see and hear and taste and touch. To what you feel. And that's what we want—isn't it? The page will force you to expand your capacity—as if that capacity were a physical thing, a muscle, a ligament you can stretch and extend with regular use—for astonishment.

One summer when my son spent a month at a sleepaway arts camp, I picked him up along with a friend of his and took them to lunch. We drove down a dirt road, away from the camp—a series of wooden shacks with hand-lettered wooden signs attached to each door: glassblowing, ceramics, sculpture studio, clown, batik, papermaking, jewelry, weaving, radio. Campers spent their days making things: plays, music, tapestries, vases, photographs, rings, chairs. As we hit the main drag—whizzing past suburban strip malls—the two boys stared out the car window as if they'd never seen the world outside before. "Somebody built that," my son's friend said, pointing to a local hospital. And then at a statue on the town green: "Probably lots of people had to agree on that. And then somebody made it." They were astonished, these boys, seeing the familiar—even the banal—in a new light.

Of course we can't walk through our days like twelve-year-old boys who have just put on 3-D glasses. Well, maybe we can—or once in a while, maybe we should?—but if we are immersed in the work of finding expression for this life, if we wake up each morning to the possibility of discovery, not only will we have a better shot at getting something worthwhile on the page, we will simply *be* better. Too often, our capacity for awe is buried beneath layers of perfectly reasonable excuses. We feel we must protect ourselves—from hurt, disappointment, insult, loss, grief—like warriors girding for battle. A Sabbath prayer that I have carried with me for more than half my life begins like this: "Days pass and the years vanish, and we walk sightless among miracles."

We cannot afford to walk sightless among miracles. Nor can we protect ourselves from suffering. We do work that thrusts us into the pulsing heart of this world, whether or not we're in the mood, whether or not it's difficult or painful or we'd prefer to avert our eyes. When I think of the wisest people I know, they share one defining trait: curiosity. They turn away from the minutiae of their lives—and focus on the world around them. They are motivated by a desire to explore the unfamiliar. They are drawn toward what they don't understand. They enjoy surprise. Some of these people are seventy, eighty, close to ninety years old, but they remind me of my son and his friend on the day I sprung them from camp. Courting astonishment. Seeking breathless wonder.

Envy

When my first book was about to come out, my literary agent told me that she had a client whose book was ranked number three on *The New York Times* best-seller list who was obsessed with the writers who were number two and number one. At the time, I thought this was insane. But I've come to see that in the writing life, there is no *enough*. There is never enough. In the years it has taken us to produce something that might be good, we have made sacrifices. Our personal lives have suffered, or our health. We've missed anniversaries, birthdays, school plays. We've slept fitfully. We've been plagued by self-doubt, paralyzing anxiety, certainty that we've really messed up, that this road we've been traveling has finally led us to a dead end. But somehow we've overcome all that and now we have a *book*. That we're holding in our *hands*. The writer's single best moment in a book's publication isn't the great review in the *Times,* or the interview on NPR. No, the single best moment in a book's publication is when the padded envelope arrives via the big brown truck—as my son used to call it—and the UPS delivery guy marches up the front walk and hands it to you. The very first copy.

Why is this a better moment than being interviewed on NPR? Because when you tear that padded envelope open and hold your book, when you open it and feel the texture of the pages, see the elegant spine and the glossy jacket, as you fetishize this object that you've been fantasizing about for . . . well, quite possibly for your whole life, nothing has happened yet. All is possibility.

But then your book begins to make its way into the world, and it feels a bit like watching helplessly from the sidewalk as your toddler navigates Times Square. You are not in control. No one is, in fact, in control. Not your agent, not your publisher, not your editor, not the lovely booksellers fighting the good fight all over this country. There is something ineffable, wholly unpredictable—something my agent calls "magic fairy dust"—that either happens to a book, or doesn't. A few of my books have had tiny sprinklings of this fairy dust over the years—but never as much as I'd like. I could give you a list right now of the writers whose books came out at around the same time as mine, or who are at the same point in their writing lives, who have gotten more. It's hard to admit this. I didn't want to write this chapter, to tell you the truth. Because envy is an ugly, shameful thing, better shoved under the rug. Except that we all feel it. We have experienced that stomach-churning sickness, that spiritual malaise, of coveting another person's good fortune.

If you were to sit a roomful of writers down and administer a truth serum, they would divulge a short list of other writers who they secretly envy, maybe even hate. Every book's publication has, for its author, a shadow publication—a book displayed more prominently in bookstores, or better publicized, or more widely reviewed. When I was in graduate school, my mentor, Jerome Badanes, published his first novel, *The Final Opus of Leon Solomon*. The book jacket of Jerry's novel was muted, dark, almost mossy-looking, as befitted a novel about a Holocaust survivor about to commit suicide. I remember browsing through the stacks at the old Shakespeare & Company on the Upper West Side with Jerry (the bookstore and the man, both long gone now, though if I stand for long enough on the corner of Eightieth and Broadway I can conjure them) and his obsession with a particular, bright orange book jacket. The other novel, the story of a traveling carnival—was also a debut, brought out by the same publisher. It was receiving glowing reviews and selling well. And Jerry—my gentle, wise, compassionate mentor—was not happy about it. Not one little bit. That orange book was his shadow publication. It went on to be a finalist for the National Book Award.

The agony! The nagging sense of what might have been! There is always someone who, at this very moment, has more. More acclaim, more money, more access, more respect . . . I see this even when I watch my son with his middle school friends. There are girls in full bloom—girls who are the envy of their classmates, girls who are at this moment as pretty and popular as they will ever be. Boys who've had growth spurts and are practically shaving, who are envied by the smaller boys who wonder when—and if—they will ever grow. Observing them, from the sidelines of ball games and dances, I want to jump up and shout: *This isn't it! You think this is it, but it isn't! Your whole lives are ahead of you with ten thousand joys and sorrows.* Of course I say nothing. My son would kill me. But I think about this—about myself and every adult, writer or not, who makes the all-too-human mistake of comparing one life to another.

When I first learned of Buddhism's eight vissicitudes— pain and pleasure, gain and loss, praise and blame, fame and disrepute—I was taught that it is *unskillful*—that gentle Buddhist word for *fucked-up*—to compare. We will never know what's coming. We cannot peer around the bend. Envy is human, yes, but also corrosive and powerful. It is our job to pursue our own dharma and covet no one else's. And perhaps the greatest challenge of all: to recognize our shadow books and wish them well.

UNCERTAINTY

I don't know how to write a novel. I don't even know how to write the novels that I've written. Once I've finished a book—truly taken it as far as I can—I look at it with some of the same awe and incomprehension that I felt when my son was born. As he lay swaddled against me, I opened the hospital blanket and counted ten fingers, ten toes. I took in his fine blond eyebrows, eyelashes. Elbows, heels, rib cage. Ears like seashells. How had he grown inside of me? How was it possible?

When *Family History*—the most intricately structured of all my novels—was sent to me by the copy editor before its publication, she had carefully taken the book apart and noticed a structural aberration. Apparently the narrative moved between the past and the present in a complex pattern that I had strayed from once during the course of the book, and the copy editor wanted to point out this anomaly to me so that I could address it. The manuscript was covered by different colored Post-its: pink for past, green for present, yellow for what I needed to fix.

Except . . . I couldn't make sense of it. Seeing the structure of my book laid out like a map was confusing. How had

I done this? I didn't know. Did it even need fixing? I reread the book—employing every trick I knew. I read it as if I were my own benign best reader. But my book had been reduced to calculus, and I had never been very good at calculus. The structure wasn't some sort of equation that needed to add up. Pulling it apart de-animated it, made it flat and incomprehensible. I knew what I was doing as I was doing it, but once the book was finished I no longer felt like its author but, rather, as mystified by it as I was by Jacob's perfect ears. It seemed impossible to me that I'd had anything to do with its creation.

This is why, when writers who are just starting out ask me when it gets easier, my answer is never. It never gets easier. I don't want to scare them, so I rarely say more than that, but the truth is that, if anything, it gets harder. The writing life isn't just filled with predictable uncertainties but with the awareness that we are always starting over again. That everything we ever write will be flawed. We may have written one book, or many, but all we know—if we know anything at all—is how to write the book we're writing. All novels are failures. Perfection itself would be a failure. All we can hope is that we will fail better. That we won't succumb to fear of the unknown. That we will not fall prey to the easy enchantments of repeating what may have worked in the past. I try to remember that the job—as well as the plight, and the unexpected joy—of the artist is to embrace uncertainty, to be sharpened and honed by it. To be *birthed* by it. Each time we come to the end of a piece of work, we have failed as we have leapt—spectacularly, brazenly—into the unknown.

BUSINESS

Fine, fine, you might be thinking. All well and good. Uncertainty, rejection, solitude, risk, pajamas all day—this is our lot. We've learned to keep good sentences in our ears. To protect our time, work regular hours. But what about the business? We hear that it's important to go to book parties and writing conferences to make connections. To write a book that has a hook. And to have, you know, thousands of Facebook and Twitter followers. And Pinterest. Goodreads. A presence. A platform.

Excuse me while I throw up a little. I don't want to write about this. I really don't, because like most writers I don't like thinking about business, or talking about business, or being aware of business at all. *Writing career* is an oxymoronic phrase. Writers are notoriously pathetic when it comes to money. Have you ever watched a group of us try to divide up the check after dinner? All those credit cards and dollar bills piled in the middle of the table? The tipsy suggestion that the waiter (himself quite possibly a struggling writer) divide it by seven, except for the bar bill, which should only be divided by four, and then add a 20 percent tip?

Also, platform is one of my all-time least favorite words, unless it's attached to the sole of a very cool shoe. I'm not fond of networking, either. It seems a calculating and manipulative way of choosing who one hangs out with. And hooks? Hooks are for coats, and even then, only in winter.

But the fact is that I have managed to support myself and my family as a writer for the past twenty years. Through a precarious and ever-evolving combination of book advances, foreign sales, movie options, royalties, screenwriting, speaking engagements, ghost writing, essays and journalism for magazines, book reviews, the odd corporate writing job, and teaching in academic institutions, retreat centers, as well as privately. Oh, yes, and I do have a Web site—though it doesn't contribute financially—and a fair number of Facebook friends and followers on Twitter.

It might seem to you that all this has been the result of a methodically carried-out plan. Or any plan at all. But I planned none of it. Almost everything that has happened in my writing life has been the result of keeping my head down and doing the work. My work led to publication. To teaching jobs. To magazine assignments. To whatever it is I've ever done—including founding a writers' conference. If I had tried to plan any of it, none of it would have happened—of that I am quite certain. And I couldn't have planned it because I couldn't have *envisioned* it. I wasn't thinking about a career. I was thinking about one book at a time.

I often tell my students—especially the ones who are impatient—that good work will find its way. When the work is ready, everything else will fall into place. I know you're sitting there, shaking your head. You don't believe me. Someone named Bookalicious, whom you follow on Twitter, who has never published a word in her life, has shared her fourteen social media strategies for writers. You're back to contemplating platforms and hooks again. You may imagine that there's a magic key that will unlock the door and all the secrets of well-published writers will come tumbling out. But I'll bet you that just about any contemporary writer you admire has never spent a single moment thinking about what their platform or hook might be.

If you work hard—with focus, diligence, integrity, honesty, optimism, and courage—on your own tiny corner of the tapestry, you just might produce something good. And if you produce something good, other writers will help you. They'll call their agents, their editors. They'll write letters on your behalf. Your teacher will lift you up on her shoulders. She will hold you aloft so that you can catch hold, so you can have the same chance she's had. Believe me. Nothing will make her happier.

NEXT

Coming to the end of writing a book is bittersweet. It must be a bit like seeing your kid off to college. You *want* your kid to go to college. You're pleased that you've raised an independent person. You marvel that this tall, complex creature is what's become of that lima-bean-sized blur you first saw on a sonogram eighteen years earlier. The printout from that sonogram is still tucked in the back of your bedside table. How have eighteen years gone by? You pack boxes, cart computer and stereo equipment, help set up a dorm room, and then you get into your car, put your head on the steering wheel, and weep.

If you have done your job—as a parent, as a writer—you've thrown your whole heart into this. And now your job is done. And you are bereft. A writer who has finished a book is an empty nester. What now? Whenever I have found myself in this condition, I always promise myself that this time, *this time,* I will do what Anthony Trollope did each time he finished a novel. He drew a line across the page beneath his final sentence—and then he started a new one. No time to think.

No time to mull over all the reasons why not. He just simply . . . kept going.

But I never do. That was Trollope's rhythm, not mine. Many of us need time between books whether we like it or not. When I finish a book, I'm depleted. All the concerns that I kept at bay while working on the book now march back into my consciousness. *Remember us?* A mild depression settles in, surprising me. It surrounds me like a fine mist and before I know it the world is unapprehendable. At precisely the moment that I am free to go back into civilization and stay a while, I feel, instead, more isolated than I do when I spend days and days speaking to no one. Once again, I feel trapped inside myself, as if someone has pressed the mute button. What do I feel? What do I think? When I'm not writing, I don't know.

I've tried many remedies for this between-books funk. I tell myself that I should use this time to relax, think, catch up on paperwork, give myself time off. But the only remedy—the only cure—for the writer is writing. It isn't about the project, it's about the practice. Whether in the midst of a serious piece of work or just taking notes, the page is where we come to meet ourselves. Most of us can't tolerate extended breaks. We are reminded how lousy, how out of touch we feel when we're away from the page. So as you come to the end, promise yourself—as I am promising myself—that you will sit down tomorrow, and the next day, and the next. Not to start something new. Not with the expectations or fantasies of what you might (or might not) accomplish. But to stay engaged with the practice of writing.

For eighty years, Pablo Casals, one of the greatest cellists who ever lived, began his day in the same manner. "I go to the piano and I play two Preludes and Fugues of Bach. It fills me with awareness of the wonder of life, and with a feeling of the incredible marvel of being a human being."

STILL WRITING

My friend Mark, a sculptor whose large-scale works in granite and marble have been commissioned by Stanford University and Penn State, whose pieces are in some of the most prominent art collections in the country, and who is a well-respected professor at the New York Academy of Art, pulled me aside at a dinner party.

"Somebody just asked me if I was still doing my sculpture thing," he said.

I laughed.

"I'm serious," he said. "How was I supposed to respond? 'Are you still doing that brain surgery thing?'"

225

I thought of all the times that I've been asked if I'm still writing. I've been asked this by acquaintances and strangers, even by fans, readers of mine. *Still writing?* It always felt, to me, like a shameful thing that I was being asked this—that surely if I had written more books, won more awards, made more money, was better known, I wouldn't be dealing with this question. *Still writing?* Over the years, I've assumed there must be a point at which this would cease to be asked. After two books? Five? Seven? After being interviewed on NPR? The *Today Show*? *Oprah,* for gods sake? Though I felt protective of my friend, it was a relief—ridiculous though it was—to hear that he had to deal with the same question. As if he might have outgrown it. Changed course. Gone into law—or opened a fish store—instead.

I've asked around, and discovered that every artist and writer I know contends with a version of this question. It's asked of writers who are household names. It's asked of photographers whose work hangs in the Museum of Modern Art. It's asked of stage actors who have won Tonys. Of poets whose work is regularly published in the finest journals. No one who spends her life creating things seems exempt from it. *Still writing?* Oh, and I'm pretty sure that the person asking it means no harm. It's just an awkward stab at social chitchat. But best to stick with the weather, or the miseries of the college admissions process, or the deliciousness of the soup.

Still writing? I usually nod and smile, then quickly change the subject. But here is what I would like to put down my fork and say: Yes, yes, I am. I will write until the day I die, or until I am robbed of my capacity to reason. Even if my fingers were to clench and wither, even if I were to grow deaf or blind, even if I were unable to move a muscle in my body save for the blink of one eye, I would still write. Writing saved my life. Writing has been my window—flung wide open to this magnificent, chaotic existence—my way of interpreting everything within my grasp. Writing has extended that grasp by pushing me beyond comfort, beyond safety, past my self-perceived limits. It has softened my heart and hardened my intellect. It has been a privilege. It has whipped my ass. It has burned into me a valuable clarity. It has made me think about suffering, randomness, good will, luck, memory, responsibility, and kindness, on a daily basis—whether I feel like it or not. It has insisted that I grow up. That I evolve. It has pushed me to get better, to *be* better. It is my disease and my cure. It has allowed me not only to withstand the losses in my life but to alter those losses—to chip away at my own bewilderment until I find the pattern in it. Once in a great while, I look up at the sky and think that, if my father were alive, maybe he would be proud of me. That if my mother were alive, I might have come up with the words to make her understand. That I am changing what I can. I am reaching a hand out to the dead and to the living and the not yet born. So yes. Yes. Still writing.

ACKNOWLEDGMENTS

Teaching creative writing has sustained me in countless ways. It has taught me the art of close reading. It has shown me that a group of serious students around a workshop table can become its own kind of sacred community. It has forced me to show up on time in grown-up clothes. For taking a chance on a young writer way back when, my gratitude to Alan Zeigler at Columbia University, who gave me my first job. Thanks too, to E. L. Doctorow at NYU and Robert Polito at The New School. To two dear writer friends, Mary Morris and John Markus, each of whom gave this book a close and valuable read. To all of my students, past and present, but particularly those in my long-standing private workshop. To my former student and dear friend and coconspirator Hannah Tinti, who helped create The Sirenland Writers' Conference. To Antonio and Carla Sersale, who allow us to hold the conference each year in their magical hotel, Le Sirenuse. To Jim and Karen

Shepard, John Burnham Schwartz, Ron Carlson, Peter Cameron, Susan Orlean, and Karen Russell, who are the world's best colleagues. To my wonderful agent Jennifer Rudolph Walsh, and to Elisabeth Schmitz, extraordinary editor, my deepest appreciation. And finally, everything begins and ends with my husband, Michael Maren, and our son, Jacob. Loves of my life.